Jayne Reading, 17

Scott Qualls, 13

Chip Myers, 7

David Burrus, 13

Kim Volskay, 17

Kari McKenzie, 15

Jodi Allen, 12

Brenda Gelder, 1

Written &

April Clore, 11

Heather McCarty, 7

David McAdoo, 10

Cashel Mack, 1

Karen Kerber, 12

Tami Cottrell, 12

Kathy Ryan, 13

Ryan Williams, 11

Illustrated by...

a revolutionary two-brain approach
for teaching students how to write
and illustrate amazing books.

David Melton

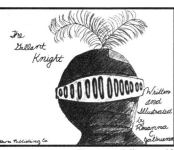

Rosanna Jalbuena, 12

Alicia Stubbs, 11

Jason Rath, 11

Jennifer Hill, 6

LANDMARK EDITIONS, INC.
Kansas City, Missouri

TO TERESA

whose valuable assistance and
development of materials for the Workshops
and whose constructive creativity in
teaching and working with the students
have affected their lives and mine in
positive ways.

International Standard Book Number: 0-933849-00-1

Library of Congress Catalog Card Number: 85-50637

© 1985 by David Melton. All rights reserved.

First Edition, First printing, October, 1985.

Landmark Editions, Inc.
1420 Kansas Avenue
Kansas City, Missouri 64127

Printed in the United States of America.

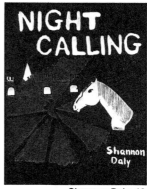

Shannon Daly, 13

Kay Henderson

Betty Lowrey

Chip Myers, 7

Billy Paronto, 11

The Melton Method

a revolutionary two-brain approach for teaching students how to write and illustrate amazing books.

David Melton is one of the most versatile and prolific talents on the literary and art scenes today. His literary works span the gamut of factual prose, analytical essays, newsreporting, magazine articles, features, short stories, poetry and novels in both the adult and juvenile fields. In the last eighteen years, twenty-four of his books have been published, several of which have been translated into a number of languages.

In WRITTEN & ILLUSTRATED BY...WORKSHOPS, conducted by Mr. Melton nationwide, more than 1,400 students from six to eighty-two years of age have written and illustrated original books. Since the publication of his book, WRITTEN & ILLUS-TRATED BY..., thousands of other students are creating wonderful books of their own.

Mr. Melton is now Creative Coordinator of Landmark Editions, Inc., a publishing company established to encourage and celebrate the creativity of students. Having already published two books by students: WALKING IS WILD, WEIRD AND WACKY, by twelve-year-old Karen Kerber; and THE DRAGON OF ORD, by fourteen-year-old David McAdoo, Landmark has initiated THE NATIONAL WRITTEN & ILLUS-TRATED BY...AWARDS CONTEST FOR STUDENTS who wish to submit original books.

To obtain printed Rules, Guidelines, and Entry Forms for the CONTEST, send a self-addressed, stamped envelope, to:

Landmark Editions, Inc.
1420 Kansas Avenue
Kansas City, Missouri   64127

The Melton Method

It has been scientifically proven that within each of our heads we have two brains. One brain is responsible for academic skills — reading, writing, speaking, and mathematics — and it maintains our sense of time and logic. The other brain controls our creative side. It is responsible for holistic, nonverbal, intuitive and visionary functions.

The Melton Method of teaching students to write and illustrate original books utilizes the functions of both the academic and creative brains.

Deadlines are structured in specific ways and time frames are organized to allow students to automatically switch their thinking processes into the appropriate right brain or left brain mode.

The students are presented precise information about book development and format. They are taught professional editorial skills, basic layout techniques and bindery procedures. And most importantly, they are offered the freedom to create in a positive and friendly environment.

Students who are convinced they suffer from "writer's block," soon find themselves writing creative prose and poetry with skill and imagination.

Students who swear they "can't draw a straight line!" are amazed to discover that not only **can** they draw and paint, but their drawings and paintings are often of professional caliber.

The truth is, children and adults are not twice as creative as we might suppose them to be. They are a thousand times more creative than we dare to dream.

Creativity is one of the most important and vital functions of human beings. We dream, we scheme, we vocalize and we design throughout the course of our every day and every night.

Contrary to popular belief, it is easy to turn on students to writing and illustrating, because the urge to create is so powerful and so accessible. We long, pine, desire and wish to express ourselves in color and line, in word and in song. Creativity is not only an intellectual pursuit — it is our spiritual and emotional quest.

One does not have to provide motivation by force or mandate. As teachers, our function is not to *"turn on"* students to creative pursuits, because children are born *"turned on"* with the urge to create. Our job is to utilize and expand their range of creativity with positive instruction, coupled with an abundance of *"oohs"* and *"aahs."* We must never stifle their confidence with *"no's"* and *"don'ts"* and *"can'ts"* and *"won'ts."* We must be ever diligent in nourishing the growth of their talents and skills.

—David Melton

The Melton Method

The Melton Method of utilizing both the academic and the creative brains of students in their development of books is so innovative it sets the mind racing. Seeing is believing — My students' writing and artistic skills improved immediately and the excitement students gained in their own creative efforts was electric. This is one of the most positive approaches to teaching I've ever experienced.

—Jean Tucker
Journalism and English Instructor
Allen County Community College

WRITTEN & ILLUSTRATED BY... is definitely on target for school objectives in basic communication skills. By creating an end product, the process of writing and illustrating books does for language arts what a science fair does for science curriculum. It combines the practice of countless skills into a tangible outcome which can be proudly examined, discussed, displayed and retained.

—Marge Hagerty
Library Media Specialist
Chinn Elementary School
Park Hill District

Thanks to The Melton Methods, many of our students' lives have been touched — and changed — as a result of writing and illustrating wonderful books. Their creativity has been released and they believe in themselves as never before.

—Kaye Anderson, Ph.D.
Southeast Missouri State University

WRITTEN & ILLUSTRATED BY... WORKSHOPS have been an overwhelming success. Students were highly motivated to produce work of professional quality. They learned they could accomplish far more than they believed they were capable of when they received qualified instruction and the freedom to develop their own ideas.

—Nancy Polette
Professor of Education
The Lindenwood Colleges

WRITTEN & ILLUSTRATED BY... exceeds the expectations of anyone wishing to write and illustrate a book. Mr. Melton's practical methods of arousing the creative brain is a unique experience that has the potential of becoming an effective tool for teaching in the future.

—Kathleen Patterson
Art Instructor
Allen County Community College

Photos by Alan Hagman

Acknowledgments

A number of teachers and parents who are vitally interested in providing creative learning experiences for students have made major contributions to the success of the WRITTEN & ILLUSTRATED BY . . . WORKSHOPS and to the development of this book.

I am most grateful to:

Nancy Polette, Professor, The Lindenwood Colleges, St. Charles, Missouri, who started the whole process by asking me to develop a workshop to teach children how to write and illustrate books.

Connie Vilott and Dr. Gail Williams who urged me to test the methods in the Independence, Missouri summer school.

Dr. Kaye Anderson, Ophelia Gilbert, Dr. Carl Grigsby, Linda Hammer, Linda Hartman, Norine Kerber, Rosemary Lumsden, Phil Sadler, Patricia Seward and Shirley Wurth in Missouri.

Julie Aikins, Neoma Boersma, Virginia Boyd, Adele Ferrell and Jean Tucker in Kansas.

Pat Joyce and Clarice Marshall in Texas.

Janet Doman, Susan Aisen, Bruce Hagy, Lidwina Van Dyk and Phyllis Kimmel in Pennsylvania for·sponsoring and assisting in the Workshops.

I am indebted to the four teachers who tested the manuscript in their classrooms: Marge Hagerty, Joyce Leibold, Jean Tucker and Kathleen Patterson. I appreciate their efforts and the wonderful books created by their students.

In the production of the book, I appreciate the assistance of Mildred Randolph, Nancy Melton, Teresa Melton, Kim Volskay, Kathy Ryan and Todd Melton.

I am grateful for the efforts of Robert Braden of Landmark Editions, Inc. and the splendid assistance of the staff of Uppercase, Inc.

A special thank you to the students who so generously allowed us to use their results of creative efforts for others to enjoy.

Kathy Glenn

Todd Leabo, 12

Dawn Grosser, 11

Kristen Mahrenholz, 12

Kay Hoffmeister

Contents

Laura Dentler, 14

Karen Reading

Renee Franke, 12

David Seuser

Mandy Rubow, 12

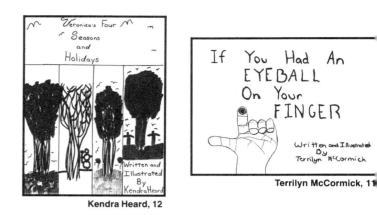

Kendra Heard, 12

Terrilyn McCormick, 11

Introduction

When I learned that David Melton was preparing a book by which teachers could teach children in schools to write and illustrate their own books, I was more than interested. I had never seen one of his WRITTEN & ILLUSTRATED BY...WORKSHOPS with children, but several summers ago, along with forty other teachers, I had participated in one of his adult creative writing courses. I knew his approach to be different — unique and rewarding — as his students were pressed into strategies which maximize use of both the academic brain and the creative brain.

When asked whether I would consider field testing his original manuscript by teaching the course to a class of elementary school students, I conferred with school administrators who quickly agreed the course would be appropriate as a pilot project for language arts curriculum. Veteran sixth-grade teacher, Joyce Leibold, felt the project fit perfectly into her goals and teaching philosophy. She offered her class which, along with some additional students, made up a total of thirty participants.

Acting as co-instructors, Mrs. Leibold and I followed the Melton manuscript closely, chapter by chapter, adjusting it only as needed to fit school practices and schedules. The manuscript indicates clearly, not only what is to be done hour by hour, but also, why the particular strategy is recommended. I often found myself re-reading the opening chapters to reaffirm reasons

for some of the students' reactions which had been clearly predicted.

Students felt a complete sense of freedom to choose topics and explore their own interests. Each book, therefore, was very different from the others in style and content, reflecting a wide variety of influences in their lives.

What developed were unique and rewarding experiences for us all which were sometimes magical, always exciting and thoroughly challenging. Although it required some extra effort from us all, challenging our ingenuity and flexibility, it produced extra dividends to every participant.

Benefits to students were numerous. Encouraged by pride in their work and the fact that their books would be available for everyone to see, they soon sought better words to replace dull phrases, corrected their own grammatical errors, improved their story lines and better understood character development. The major benefit, however, was the students' joy of achievement which was glorious to behold.

Ours was the usual cross section of learners: fast, average, slow, lazy, disabled. Given a choice, many would probably never have enrolled in such a course. All were challenged to do what they had never done before or seen done. Most felt they might write something but doubted they could illustrate it. By listening carefully to the instructions from the manuscript and by

Kevin Smith, 12

Betty Krone

Michael Hogue, 12

Craig Armstrong, 14

Leo Garcia, 12

Darren Magady, 12

Danny Harris, 11

helping and encouraging each other, they found skills they little suspected themselves of having. Frequently students from whom average work might be expected were more creative than the usual achievers. When their work was completed, all thirty students certainly walked taller among their peers.

At first I, too, wondered whether illustrating the story was all that important. Then little by little I came to see that students were analyzing their stories in order to decide which scene to illustrate, and were learning the storytelling potential of illustrations.

As we were evaluating the project before the Authors' Party, Mrs. Leibold commented that through working with her students in this kind of project, she had become better acquainted with them in a different manner than usual and had gained more respect for their potential, their standards and their sense of cooperation. It was even more apparent for me. I grew to know those students as I had never known sixth-grade students before.

WRITTEN & ILLUSTRATED BY... is definitely on target for school objectives in basic communication skills: reading, writing, spelling, grammar, listening, speaking and illustrating. It goes beyond mere comprehension and encourages the student to exercise critical judgment which is extremely important in the context of education. By creating an end product, the process of writing and illustrating books does for language arts what a science fair does for science curriculum. It com-

bines the practice of countless skills into a tangible outcome which can be proudly examined, discussed, displayed and retained.

Of course we placed each book in the library if the author wished to contribute it. Henceforth these students were "real authors." They were also invited to read their books to younger children in classrooms and to review them at a public meeting. Special copies were presented to school administrators. Under these circumstances, children become self-motivated and do want to do their best work.

The Melton approach in utilizing the functions of both the academic brain and the creative brain of students, clearly stated, offers valuable insight into other aspects of teaching and learning. What works with writing and illustrating books will surely work in other classroom situations.

I highly commend the Melton method of teaching writing and illustrating and the book which explains it so thoroughly that no teacher need have any qualms about procedures. Yes, we would enthusiastically do it again. We certainly encourage other teachers to read this fascinating book and enjoy changing the lives of students in this unforgettable way.

Marge Hagerty
Library Media Specialist
Chinn Elementary School
Park Hill District

Janell Shamet, 12

Cara Anne Caputo, 9

Jill Grant, 12

Kevin Henderson, 13

Mary Ryan, 12

The Adventures of SUPER FATS
By Tony Rennick

Tony Rennick, 14

ALBERT the ARMADILLO
written and illustrated by Sue Donaldson

Sue Donaldson

Thoughts
Written and Illustrated By John Joiner

John Joiner

be easy daddy
written and illustrated by ruthann thompson

Ruthann Thompson, 17

Video Master
Written + Illustrated by Tom Lynch, 13

Tom Lynch, 12

A Farmer's Daughter
Written and Illustrated By Susan Koenig

Susan Koenig, 14

MARVELOUS McGEE AND THE ANGRY MACHINE
written and illustrated by Julie Aikins
Chanute Publishing Co.

Julie Aikins

Hound and Goose
Written and Illustrated by Clarice Marshall

Clarice Marshall

Miss Beasley
by Khris Breitling

Khris Breitling, 13

Torn Between Two Friends
Written and Illustrated by Beth Blackwell

Beth Blackwell, 13

THE MYSTERIOUS PICTURE
WRITTEN AND ILLUSTRATED BY JULIE HAWK

Julie Hawk, 12

ACADIANA
written and illustrated by Mister Vincent Veillon

Vincent Veillon

Looking Through The Dark Stairway
Illustrated and Written by Rebecca K. Wholf

Rebecca K. Wholf, 13

JOJO FINDS A FRIEND
Written And Illustrated by: Lisa Bohanon

Lisa Bohanon, 12

That's How I Was Adopted
Written and Illustrated by Patricia Parker Witzenburg

Patricia P. Witzenburg

to imagine is to dream

written and illustrated by elyce elder

1
Students Can Write and Illustrate Amazing Books

When Given the Opportunity

I Love Words

Written and illustrated By molly-Ann Perira

Molly Ann Pereira, 6

create:

to bring into existence, make out of nothing and for the first time;

to cause to be or to produce by fiat or by mental, moral, or legal action.

If there is anything more fun than writing a book, it is illustrating it too. It is called double your pleasure, double your fun.

I love to write and illustrate books.

I think writing and illustrating are:

- tastier than steak for breakfast and cheesecake for dessert;
- as challenging as scaling Mount Everest;
- as rewarding as discovering buried treasure;
- as frustrating as completing an income tax form, yet as exhilarating as flying solo in a starliner superjet.

Writing and illustrating offer both the confinement of a prison cell and the reward of total freedom.

These activities set the mind soaring, the heart racing, make muscles tighten and fingers tingle, and cause a quickness of breath and a rush of oxygen throughout the body.

Quite simply — I happen to think creating a book is a WOW!

I believe I am one of the luckiest of people because I am allowed to do the kind of work I love best and publishers pay me to do it. For me it is a splendid arrangement.

But I'll tell you a secret — if I didn't get paid to write and illustrate books, I would do it anyway — because it is so much fun.

If there is any activity nearly as exciting as writing and illustrating a book, it is observing others creating literary and visual delights.

WRITTEN & ILLUSTRATED BY...

During the past five years, I have conducted WRITTEN & ILLUSTRATED BY...WORKSHOPS in various cities, from Houston, Texas to Philadelphia, Pennsylvania. In these Workshops, more than fourteen hundred children and adults have created wonderful books. What began as a course

Susan M. Haynie, 10

book:

a formal written document;

a collection of written sheets of skin or tablets of wood or ivory;

a continuous roll of parchment or a strip of parchment creased between columns and folded like an accordion;

a collection of written, printed, or blank sheets fastened together along one edge and usually trimmed at the other edges to form a single series of uniform leaves, a collection of folded sheets bearing printing or writing that have been cut, sewn, and usually bound between covers into a volume.

Lea Carney, 14

specifically designed for students from twelve to sixteen years of age has been broadened and adapted to include a wider spectrum of participants. To my knowledge, the youngest students to attend the Workshop were six years old and the oldest was seventy-two. I have also conducted Workshops for groups of brain-injured children and young adults.

While these students were learning book format and production, they taught me extremely important pieces of information.

I now know that children and adults are not twice as creative as we might suppose them to be; they are a thousand times more creative than we dared dream.

I am convinced many people who think they can't write, not only **can** write but their work can quickly and easily be transformed into the professional range.

Many people who swear they "can't draw a straight line," when given the opportunity and the encouragement, can draw and paint with extraordinary skills and imagination.

In the proper setting, students will correct and rewrite their stories on their own without being badgered. They will check the spelling of words and learn the rules of punctuation without being prodded or threatened. They will create all elements of their books not because they are told to do so, but because they are eager to do all of these things.

Books by Students?
How Cute!

When friends or colleagues ask what I've been doing during the summer, and I tell them I've been teaching children to write and illustrate books, I see them force Cheshire cat smiles. I hear them say, "How nice. I bet their books are really cute." Their demeanors reveal the prevailing attitudes of "little heads, little minds." I'm sure they envision stories of gingerbread men and childish cartoons.

The more honest ones come right out with it. "What on earth would children have to write about?" they bluntly ask.

The answer is simple and direct — children and teenagers write about the very same things adults write about. Better still, they write about the same topics professional writers write about. In fact, their skills in writing often match the standards of professional writing and their insights are just as profound. When given the freedom to explore, without hesitation, young people tackle any genre in both fiction and non-fiction.

They write adventure stories, fairytales, mysteries, fantasies, horror stories, biographies, autobiographies, westerns, sports stories, historical dramas, romance novels, whodunits, psychological thrillers, self-help books and plays. They write of social problems, ecology considerations, racial injustices and periods of self-evaluation. They examine political issues and write about the rights of the handicapped and the courage of the individual.

The books created in the Workshops are not developed from supplied formulae. Participants are allowed to venture into any genre they choose. No restrictions are placed on subject matter. The choice of what to write about belongs to the students, as does the choice of art medium for illustrating their books (water color, felt tips, ink, pencil, etc.). The only restrictions placed on the books are in regard to size and number of pages, and we'll discuss the reasons for these stipulations in a later chapter.

One might suppose those students who enroll in the WRITTEN & ILLUSTRATED BY...WORKSHOPS are the ''cream of the crop'' — those students who are in the upper ten percentile academically. It is an assumption I made in the beginning but, to my surprise, such has not been the case. My first group of twenty-seven students was composed of a mixed bag of ages, abilities and work habits. On the first day, I learned that during registration exceptions had been made — several students were younger than I had specified and some were older. Although I had insisted that the students be hand-picked according to their abilities, I discovered the first twenty-five had been enrolled on a first come, first served basis. The two extra students had been admitted for political reasons rather than by skills. I would soon learn that group was a very accurate prediction of the future groups to come.

In fact, it occurs to me, I have never conducted the Workshop for any group for which it was initially designed. I have never once had a group composed of twenty-five students who were from twelve to sixteen years of age. They have all been assembled with exceptions and exceptions to the exceptions. And although they are not usually from the upper ten or even twenty percentile in academic standing, somehow or someway we do seem to get the ''cream of the crop'' in creative and inventive individuals.

Mothers and fathers of some of my students tell me, ''I don't know why my child wanted to enroll in this Workshop, because he (or she) doesn't do very well in school.''

Some parents say, ''I don't know what's going on here. My child hates to do homework, but last night she (or he) stayed up until after two o'clock working on the book.''

The three teachers who taught classes from the original manuscript of this book were amazed to discover that not only were the top students putting extra time and effort into their books, but many of the lower students who the teachers thought would drift through the project were suddenly showing real interest. By the end of the course, many of these lower students had developed some of the best books.

''I have no doubt,'' Marge Hagerty says, ''out of thirty students, we had five miracles. We discovered that five of our students could do work far beyond anything we had seen them do in the regular classroom. We found one of our students who hardly participates in most classroom activities is probably a genius. It's really exciting to see students work beyond their own grade level. But when you find a sixth-grade student who usually works below his grade level suddenly write material that would put many college graduates to shame—now that's really amazing!''

Down with the Talent Myth —

As a teacher, my constant fear is I will fail to offer the needed encouragement, or somehow miss seeing an extraordinary talent or not recognize that spark of genius in one of my students.

Do you know any teacher who can look at the faces in a new class and determine which ones are talented and which ones are not? Well, I don't. And I can't.

However, I have a formula that is certainly as good as any and I'm sure better than most. I walk into each Workshop with the firm conviction that each and every student, no matter what age, size, shape or color he or she may be, has the potential for creative genius. Within days, some-

written and illustrated by
missy Krehbiel

Missy Krehbiel, 12

LOOKING THROUGH THE DARK STAIRWAY
— Rebecca K. Wholf, 13

MUST WEREWOLVES EAT RARE STEAK? — Christion Schulte, 15

talent:

the abilities, powers, and gifts bestowed upon a man or a woman, a boy or a girl, natural endowments;

a special innate or developed aptitude for an expressed or implied activity usually of a creative or artistic nature;

general intelligence or mental power, ability.

Birds do not fly
because they have wings.
Birds have wings
because they need to fly.
First there is a need,
Then there is the facility.

It is just as true in the case of talent:

People do not create
because they have talent.
People have talent
because they have the need to create.
First there is the need,
Then there is the facility.

THE TINY TRIO AND THE CASE OF THE MISSING MOZZARELLA — Darren Magady, 12

BEYOND THE WISHING WELL
— Virginia Sheets, 15

Creativity is a child's most valuable asset because he has not yet learned all the popular views and answers. And his creativity is vital to our society.

— Jean E. Laird
  Creativity: Your Greatest Gift to
  Your Child

times even hours, these wonderful students prove I am right.

Contrary to what most people believe, talent is not a rare commodity possessed only by a select few, but comes in large abundance, barely hidden beneath the surface of almost everyone, waiting to be recognized and released. With the proper encouragement, talent bursts forth with amazing regularity.

The misuse of the word, "talent," has overshadowed the way we assess creativity. We tend to believe people create because they have talent. We even go a step beyond and propose that people are either born with the ability to be creative or they are not. Nothing could be farther from the truth.

Who would have known that Marilyn Horne was a talented singer if she had not worked to create that discipline called an operatic voice?

If Salvador Dali had not created those marvelous plastic and weightless shapes, who would have known the man possessed artistic talent?

And if Truman Capote had not served BREAKFAST AT TIFFANY'S or reminded us of A CHRISTMAS MEMORY, or chilled us IN COLD BLOOD, how should we have known he was a "talented" writer?

The fact is so clear. We are not recognizing talent at all; what we are observing are types of skills. It is only after people create that we begin to recognize their talents — not before.

More Students Are Talented Than We Might Suppose

When conducting the WRITTEN & ILLUSTRATED BY...WORK-SHOPS, I see my function very clearly. It is not my job or even my desire to seek out talents. It is my job to find at what levels of skills each student is functioning, whether that student is a child or adult, and to help that student to accelerate his or her abilities to the next level and beyond. If I find one is functioning at a fifth-grade level, I want to move him or her to a sixth-grade range, or into the high school range, or into the professional range. I want to see their abilities improve so dynamically and so quickly they feel they might explode from the excitement.

Anyone can write and anyone can draw. Writers can become terrific artists; artists can become fantastic writers — not in fifty years or a thousand-and-one nights, but in minutes and days. It will not be my words or your words that will convince students they can write and illustrate; it is the improvement they see in their work that will ignite their interests. Of course, that's why my students return to the Workshop each day — not to see me, or laugh at my jokes or listen to what I have to say; they return because they realize there's a very gifted and talented person inside each of them who won't wait another minute or another day to be set free. The price of that freedom is in the doing. The price of discovering these talents is in the courage to create.

In the dedication of his book, one student wrote:

Mr. Melton saw more in me than I knew I had. When I tried to reach those goals, I found out he was right. I am more than I thought I was. I am more creative than I thought I ever could be. I am a writer. And I am an illustrator. I am a creative person.

In one Workshop, a teacher and her student of the previous year, a twelve-year-old girl, were participants. The first day the teacher drew me aside and said in secretive tones, "I have never been so shocked in my life — I can't believe that girl enrolled in the Workshop. She never gets her work done on time. She can't draw and she certainly can't write. She responds very negatively to suggestions. And her mother can be a real 'witch.' Don't be surprised if the girl drops out in a day or two and her mother comes flying in here wanting her money returned."

When I read the girl's story on Tuesday evening, I wondered if the teacher had the girl confused with someone else, because the child's first draft was beautifully constructed and extremely well written. And when she began to develop her illustrations, I found not only could she draw, but she had a marvelous flair for color and design. As for taking suggestions, she was very receptive and became very excited about the improvements in her work. As for never completing anything on time, she kept in pace with the rest of the group and was ready to assemble her book on Friday.

The Workshop on Fridays is a room transformed into assembly lines of gluing, binding and trimming. At about one o'clock, someone finally finishes gluing and is ready for pages to be stitched and trimmed. As soon as the book is trimmed, within seconds, the book jacket is wrapped around it and we have a finished product. Immediately, I always ask everyone to stop working and gather around the table. I then announce that our publishing company, which has only been in existence for five days, has produced its first book. I hold up the book for everyone to see and the writer/illustrator receives a round of well-deserved applause. While all the books receive such attention, there is no doubt the first one reaps more than its fair share.

During the Workshop attended by this twelve-year-old girl, I had made up my mind that if at all possible, come Friday, her book would be the first off the line. If that is considered cheating, then fine. But I happened to think it was important for her to be first.

As the books were nearing completion, I could see hers might not be ready first, but it would surely be in the first ten. When other students gave me their books for review, I purposely sent them back to check their pages again and make sure all the corners were properly pasted (which would have to be done anyway). But the moment this girl's pages were glued, I rushed her materials to the table, stitched and trimmed the pages, wrapped the jacket around the book and summoned everyone to gather. Making my customary speech, I held up the book to receive the enthusiastic applause and cheers. Pretending I had forgotten the words of warning, I carefully avoided looking directly at the teacher who was standing at the back of the group.

Then the girl did a wonderful thing. She gave me a quick hug, took her book and walked straight to the teacher and handed the book to her, as if to say, "You see, I am more than you could see."

No one else in the room was aware of the drama of that scene except the girl and me — and hopefully the teacher.

With an open mind, willing to ignore preconceived notions, and with faith in the creative spirit of children, many of us may be fortunate enough to escape the experience of having a student walk up to us, show us an outstanding achievement and even say aloud, "Look, I am more than you could see."

I never want any student, whether he or she is a child or an adult, to ever conclude, "There is more to me than Mr. Melton ever supposed."

Michelle Mettlach, 12

teach:

show, guide, direct, to cause to know a subject;

to cause to know how to do something; show how; to accustom to some action or attitude;

to direct as an instructor, guide the studies of, conduct through a course of studies, give instruction;

to impart knowledge;

to present in a classroom lecture or discussion;

to instruct in the rules, principles or practice.

HOUND AND GOOSE
— Clarice Marshall

Mark Brandau, 11

educate:

to bring up (as a child or animal), rear;

to develop (as a person) by fostering to varying degrees the growth or expansion of knowledge, wisdom, desirable qualities of mind or character, physical health, or general competence especially by a course of formal study or instruction;

provide or assist in providing with knowledge or wisdom, moral balance, or good physical conditions especially by means of a formal education, provide with formal schooling;

to train by formal instruction and supervised practice especially in a trade, skill, or profession;

to provide with information;

to bring about an improvement in or refinement of.

AGE OF AQUARIUS
— Brendan Shepherd, 13

Instead, I would hope students believe, "He sees more in me than I ever supposed — and he is right!"

The Methods Are Simple, Direct and They Work!

By utilizing the methods of tapping the resources of both the academic and creative brains of the students, as outlined in this book, there is no reason why your class cannot achieve equal and even superior results. These are surefire methods for unleashing the creative forces of students. These methods are easy. They are simple. They are direct. They are immediate. They are well-formulated. They are well-documented. And even better — these methods work!

Although there are certain advantages in students giving an all-out effort in the production of their book projects without the interruption of other classes and subjects, there are equal advantages in allowing them to work on their books during shorter sessions with the overall production and the completion of their books being projected over an extended number of days.

In fact, when I look at the outline of lesson plans, it is obvious that the WRITTEN & ILLUSTRATED BY...WORKSHOPS can be scheduled by hours as well as days. The Workshops can be integrated into the school-day routine with very little effort.

Get Ready To Blast Off!

The remainder of this book will address itself to the CANS and the WHYS and the HOWS of discovering, developing and channeling the creative potentials in not only one or two children or adults at a time, but in rooms full of people.

If you want to turn your class into a dynamic learning center, it can be done in minutes.

If you would like to turn on students to the importance of sentence structure and punctuation, now's your chance.

If you would like to feel the electrifying experience of students discovering how creative they really are and see them gain respect for the creativity of others, now's your opportunity.

We are about to embark upon a journey into an exciting universe of time and space that is filled with enormous opportunities and uncharted imagination. It will be a glorious trip of high adventure and broadening insights. We will traverse the light years of millions of dreams and ignite billions of brain cells. This journey holds the promise of changing your classroom forever and allows you to look at your students with enlightened interest. As a teacher and as a person, you may never again be the same.

Now then, if you have yawned or dozed off during this last paragraph, you might as well close these pages and go to sleep — this is not a book for you.

However, if you feel charged with excitement and ready to go, then fasten your seatbelt because we are about to enter the final countdown and will soon be ready to blast-off!

2

Two Brains for the Price of One

The Academic/Creative Approach

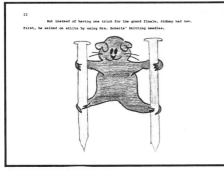

SIDNEY THE SUPER PIG
— Laura Dentler, 14

The brain is like the earth. The earth is big but the brain is bigger. The earth is one of many planets within the universe but the brain is cosmic. As far as Man can reach out into the universe so can he reach just as far into the brain. The brain is not only information — it is imagination. It is both precise and precious. It is both a storage place and a source of information. It is both fact and fiction. Yesterday and today — the past and the future.

— Raymundo Veras, M.D.
Children of Dreams —
Children of Hope

When students write their own books, their drawing and painting skills improve because through creation and examination of characters and structures of the plot, they can better understand the style and mood of the story, which ultimately enhances their illustrations.

By the same token, having your students illustrate their books transports their thinking from the written materials and moves them into considering their stories from another viewpoint. While working on their illustrations, many students begin to see new possibilities in their stories and will, on their own, expand and refine their work. And as their illustrations begin to take shape, the students gain respect for the visual quality of their work. They do not want to see typographical errors detract from the appearance of their books. Now the margins and the paragraphing and the commas and the periods become important to them. I promise you this is true.

It was sometime before I learned how important having students illustrate their written work really is. Through this process I was unknowingly sending a loud and clear signal to their creative brains.

Unraveling the Riddles of the Human Brain

How is it possible to discuss learning, teaching and creativity without regard for that organ of learning and creativity — the brain? It is not. To do so would be like discussing the circulatory system without mentioning the heart. It would be like discussing the ocean without mentioning water. It would be like discussing our solar system without mentioning the sun.

It amazes me that in vast volumes of books which are published on the subjects of education, academic achievement and learning, so few of them even mention the brain. They so often read as if hearing is a function of the ears, that reading is a function of the eyes, that talking is a function of the mouth, that writing is a function of the hands, that coordination is

The human brain is protected by a life support system that favors it over every other organ in the body. Encased in bone to shield its soft tissue, the brain is bathed in cerebrospinal fluid to protect it against impact. Although it makes up only 2 percent of the body's total weight, it receives a highly disproportionate share of nutriments. Even in cases of malnutrition, it has been found that although a child may weigh half the normal weight, his brain may be only 15 percent below the norm.

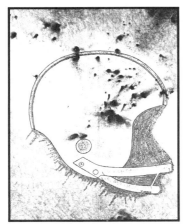

GEE, IF THE GUYS COULD SEE ME NOW! — Tim Herod, 17

The shiny, wrinkled jelly of the human brain . . . is more intricate and effective than any other work of nature. Whether we are awake or asleep, its electrochemical network of ten billion nerve cells maintains a ceaseless activity, running the myriad functions of the body (breathing alone requires the complex coordination of 90 muscles) and analyzing raw sense data from the outside world. . . . The brain can process hundreds of bits of information at a time, and it can sedulously distinguish between reality and memory and fantasy. It has even developed the capacity to control — at least in part — the very drives and emotions that it spawns.

— Adrian Hope
The Brain

a function of the body and that feeling is a function of the skin. It is as if these authors are asserting that a child's ears have to learn to understand words, that a child's mouth has to learn how to speak, that a child's hand has to learn how to write, that a child's body has to learn to turn somersaults and that a child's skin has to learn how to touch. Isn't it obvious that hands, mouths, eyes, ears, noses and thoughts do not learn anything? It is the brain that learns. It is the brain that thinks. It is the brain that must be taught. Without a functioning brain, a hand is no more than a piece of meat, eyes and ears are useless receptors, the mouth is a silent voice box. Without the brain there is no learning. Without the brain there is no student.

When we say we are teaching students, we are in reality programming their brains. Learning depends on how their brains accept the input of information and how that information is organized and assimilated. In recent years we have discovered exciting insights about the complexities of brain activities which answer a number of questions in regard to not only the thinking processes of students, but our own.

Very Interesting, but What Does It Mean?

Have you noticed some students who are able to pass spelling tests with flying colors often misspell the same words when they are writing a story or a poem?

Have you ever wondered why you have a complete sense of time while dealing with factual matters, but when you are engaged in creative pursuits, you lose all track of minutes ticking by?

Have you ever written a story or an article and, when you review it the following day, you find sections you don't recall writing?

Have you ever noticed when writing, those first three or four paragraphs are laborious and difficult, or when drawing, the first lines are often stilted and awkward? Then suddenly, everything begins to take form and shape and you discover the writing or the drawing becomes fun and effortless.

When beginning a new activity, have you ever said, ''I need time to switch gears?''

Have you ever gone home after a demanding day at work and turned on the record player to relax? Have you ever noticed the sound of music not only turns off types of rational thinking, but brings forth thoughts and types of creative ideas?

Have you ever reviewed a set of facts and figures which seem to be well-documented and orderly, but a seemingly small self from within tells you that something is wrong?

Have you ever suddenly decided that you've had enough of the everyday grind, that you simply have to go to a movie or read a suspense novel, or take some time for yourself? And when you do, what self do you mean?

Have you ever felt that hidden within your personality, either deep inside or just below the surface, there is a capacity for creativity that you have never explored or that you haven't utilized fully?

Have you ever felt instead of being one person, perhaps there are really two of you — one rational person who deals with the realities of life, and one irrational person who has sudden whims and changes of mood?

Of course you have. Most people have experienced these thoughts and situations. In the past, such experiences were termed "personality shifts," or "creative impulses," or "daydreaming," and so on. But we now know such occurrences are the result of brain functions — not the working of just **one brain,** but of **two** — a **left brain** and a **right brain.**

Left Brain — Right Brain

The **left brain** is responsible for the functions of the **right** side of our bodies; the **right brain** is responsible for the functions of the **left** side of our bodies.

It has been established that one brain controls speech patterns and the other brain controls rhythm or musical patterns.

In the past, the speech pattern side was often referred to as the **dominant side.** The other brain is usually referred to as the **subdominant side.**

If a person suffers a stroke or damage to the left brain, the right side of his or her body will be most seriously affected and vice versa. If the speech area is injured, the person may not be able to speak but may be able to sing, since tonality is centered in one brain and verbality in the other. But if the tonality area of one's brain is injured, the person may be able to speak without difficulty but will not be able to hum or sing a melody.

A quick experiment will show you how this works. Stop reading for a moment and try to recite the lyrics of a song without humming the tune. You'll find it is quite difficult to do because you have learned the song in your "tonality" of the subdominant brain and, without the tune, you are asking your "speech" dominant brain to recite the lines. Since your dominant brain has also heard the lines, it will respond with some of the stanzas — but start humming the tune and the words will start flowing from your subdominant brain without effort.

Although widespread discussion and much attention have been given to the functions of the two brains, the results of scientific research have been available for several decades. During the 1950s, Dr. Temple Fay, the renowned neurosurgeon, did extensive research on the two-brain theory. A colleague of Fay, Glenn Doman, a physical therapist, initiated innovative methods of therapies for brain-injured children which intensified the presentation of information into the dominant hemisphere and developed programs which strengthened the neurological development of these children.

These methods received much attention in the news media and a number of articles and books have been written about them, including several of my own. The programs of therapy became commonly referred to as the Doman-Delacato methods — the crawling and creeping programs. And the Institutes for the Achievement of Human Potential gained both international acclaim and a certain amount of criticism, which is expected when new ideas are presented.

As I related in my first book, TODD, my wife, Nancy, and I had personal experience with the Institutes' programs because our son was brain-injured at birth. When he was eight years old, we took him out of a special education classroom and placed him on one of the Institutes' therapy programs. Assisted by over one hundred and thirty volunteers in our community who came to our home weekly to assist in Todd's "patterning" therapy, our son's condition rapidly improved.

JEREMIAH'S FLYING UNICORN
— Dawn Grosser, 11

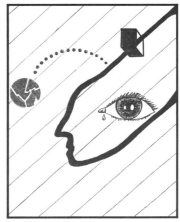

ASHES IN THE WIND
— Tim Phillips, 17

There are approximately one hundred billion cells in every child's head. At least ten billion of these are neurons of nerve cells capable of functioning as operating units of the brain. Ten billion is a difficult number to associate with reality even for an American taxpayer. To try to give some reality to this number it is helpful to know that if your child had been born before Christ and used a brand-new brain cell every ten seconds, sixty seconds a minute, sixty minutes an hour, twenty-four hours a day, three hundred and sixty-five days a year, and if that child were still alive today, he would have more than three billion neurons which he hadn't yet used.

— Glenn Doman, author
How To Teach Your Baby To Read

academic:

belonging to, or associated with an academy or school especially of higher learning;

formed by school training or associations, scholarly.

END OF LINE
— Tom Gardner, 12

creativity:

the quality of being creative, the ability to create.

THE CONFLICTING POWER
— Gary Jones, 17

creation:

the act of creating, the act of bringing into existence from nothing the universe or the world or the living and nonliving things in it;

the act or practice of making, inventing, devising, fashioning, or producing;

the presentation of a new conception in an artistic embodiment;

an original work of art or of the imagination.

Within eighteen months, he returned to school, not to a special education classroom, but to a regular class. Asking no favors or special attention, he later graduated from high school. Today, Todd is a self-sufficient adult. He has a good job, is buying his own home and is in the process of rebuilding a 1953 Studebaker. Consequently, we have had more than a casual interest in brain function, in methods of accelerating learning and in teaching processes.

Academic Brain — Creative Brain

At dinner one evening some fifteen years ago, Carl Delacato, Ed.D., mentioned something that struck me like a thunderbolt. He said he suspected there is a strong possibility the two brains are incorrectly labeled as dominant and subdominant. Instead, they should be labeled as **"academic"** and **"creative,"** the speech side being responsible for **academic** thought patterns, and the musical side responsible for **creative** patterns. In many ways, Delacato's theory of the **academic** and the **creative** brains makes good sense.

In the last few years I have had the opportunity to talk with a number of writers. The one question I am always led to ask is, "How do you write?" Uniformly, they answer they go through rituals to prepare themselves to begin. Some writers require an hour of preparation before finally writing a word. This seems to be true also of artists. It is legitimate to ask whether this time of preparation is only to sharpen pencils and stack paper, or whether it is used to get an idea. Or, is this the time required by them to switch their thought processes from the **academic** brain to the **creative** brain? It's an interesting question.

I hear so much about creative moods. Many writers and illustrators maintain the "creative mood" is, in reality, the ability to function on another level of thought patterns. Some even feel they may mentally transcend into a hypnotic state before they can create. I think there is a certain validity in those observations because I have personally found creative processes often seem to come from another plane of awareness.

I have a quirk in my work — I can never remember anything I have written. My friend, Rod McKuen, has the same quirk. He can easily sing his own songs, but even in concert, he has to read his poetry rather than trust his memory.

What does this mean? Does it mean that Rod and I have short memories? I don't think so. I can recite "I must go down to the sea again" and any number of stanzas written by other people, and I know Rod can too. Perhaps it means, then, our creative brains don't always know what our academic brains are doing and vice versa. And perhaps it means people are, indeed, schizophrenic — two people in one head — a creative person and an academic person.

Some ten years later, Dr. Roger W. Sperry, a technological psychology professor, and his team at the California Institute of Technology validated similar theories and labeled the functions of the two brains. Dr. Sperry received a Nobel Prize for the work. Sperry compared the characteristics of the two brains as follows:

A COMPARISON OF THE CHARACTERISTICS OF THE ACADEMIC BRAIN AND THE CREATIVE BRAIN

ACADEMIC

Verbal:
Using words to name, describe, define.

Analytic:
Figuring things out step-by-step and part-by-part.

Symbolic:
Using a symbol to stand for something. For example, the drawn form 👁 stands for eye, the sign + stands for the process of addition.

Abstract:
Taking out a small bit of information and using it to represent the whole thing.

Temporal:
Keeping track of time, sequencing one thing after another. Doing first things first, second things second, etc.

Rational:
Drawing conclusions based on reason and facts.

Digital:
Using numbers as in counting.

Logical:
Drawing conclusions based on logic: one thing following another in logical order — for example, a mathematical theorem or a well-stated argument.

Linear:
Thinking in terms of linked ideas, one thought directly following another, often leading to a convergent conclusion.

CREATIVE

Nonverbal:
Awareness of things, but minimal connection with words.

Synthetic:
Putting things together to form wholes.

Concrete:
Relating to things as they are, at the present moment.

Analogic:
Seeing likenesses between things — understanding metaphoric relationships.

Nontemporal:
Without a sense of time.

Nonrational:
Not requiring a basis of reason or facts — willingness to suspend judgment.

Spatial:
Seeing where things are in relation to other things and how parts go together to form a whole.

Intuitive:
Making less of insight, often based on incomplete patterns, hunches, feelings or visual images.

Holistic:
Seeing whole things all at once — perceiving the overall patterns and structures, often leading to divergent conclusions.

"The main theme to emerge . . . is that there appear to be two modes of thinking — verbal and nonverbal — represented rather separately in the left and right hemispheres, respectively," writes Dr. Sperry. ". . . our educational system, as well as science in general, tends to neglect the nonverbal for the intellect. What it comes down to is that modern society discriminates against the right hemisphere."

The Importance of Recognizing the Functions of Both Brains

If the compilation of the functions of the two brains were merely labels and could not be utilized nor affected by teaching methods, it would still be interesting. However, since brain function can be altered and dynam-

JENNIFER MEETS BUTTERCUP
— Kathy Myers

With respect to human beings, where else would you get a nonlinear computer weighing only 160 pounds, having a billion binary decision elements that can be mass produced by unskilled labor?

— Scott Crossfield
  X-15 Pilot

BECAUSE THAT'S THE WAY IT IS
— Kevin Henderson, 13

TO BECOME A WARRIOR
— Janet Moody, 14

. . . The child is curious. He wants to make sense out of things, find out how things work, gain competence and control over himself and his environment, do what he can see other people doing. He is open, receptive, and perceptive. He does not shut himself off from the strange, confused, complicated world around him. He observes it closely and sharply, tries to take it all in. He is experimental. He does not merely observe the world around him, but tastes it, touches it, hefts it, bends it, breaks it. . . .

— John Holt
  How Children Learn

ically accelerated, it should be of enormous interest to teachers and have a profound effect on teaching methods.

In her book, DRAWING ON THE RIGHT SIDE OF THE BRAIN, Dr. Betty Edwards, expounding on Dr. Sperry's findings, offers great insights in ways to improve one's abilities to draw by utilizing methods which stimulate the "creative brain."

While teachers thought it interesting that the methods improved the drawing abilities of students, they questioned whether or not other methods of affecting brain function could be utilized in improving one's writing or understanding of language. It was obvious to me they could. And these methods are so easy and so effective they make turning cartwheels and skydiving seem ordinary in comparison.

It should also be obvious schools are set up to primarily program and utilize the academic brains of students. That is not a criticism, but a fact. Public and parochial schools are designed to teach students reading, grammar and arithmetic, and how to develop analytical thinking processes, how to delineate logical progressions of facts and how to draw rational conclusions — all of which are functions of the academic brain.

One of the primary purposes of public education was and is to prepare students to be functioning adults — to be able to read directions and communicate with others, to be able to measure materials, order numbers of supplies and to properly bill for services and products, to write letters and keep necessary records, and to tell the time of day and count money are all basic requirements in employment. How well students master these skills has a direct effect on the types of employment they can obtain, and has bearing on the advancement they might achieve.

Although early educators viewed drawing, painting, music and creative writing as art forms and appreciated the outstanding accomplishments of the great artists, it was virtually concluded that, for the most part, drawing, singing or playing a musical instrument were pleasurable pastimes. It was also concluded only a few people could excel in these pursuits and even fewer could earn a decent living in those fields. So, other than in elementary school, and sometimes even then, art, music and other creative endeavors were and are pursued in separate classrooms, being often considered as lesser important school curricula and many times offered only as elective courses.

Such a system "force feeds" the academic brains of students while neglecting their creative brains. The retention of facts and figures is more easily tested, scored and measured on class curves, but creativity and the spawning of ideas are intangibles and much more difficult to evaluate — perhaps even impossible.

I am not proposing schools must give the creative brain equal time, but this brain certainly deserves more attention than it now receives.

While it is the academic brain that leads one to become an accountant, it is the use of both brains that allows people to become financiers.

While the academic brain produces the draftsman, it is the use of both brains that develops the architect and designing engineer.

While it is the academic brain that provides the vocabulary and format for reading and the grammatical knowledge for writing, it is the combined functions of both brains that create works of literature.

While the academic brain is interested in social and cultural conditions, it is the marriage with the creative brain that produces the philosopher.

While it is the academic brain that adds, subtracts, multiplies and divides numbers, it is the joining of forces with the creative brain that gives birth to new theories.

For instance, in 1905 a young mathematician named Albert Einstein was riding on a streetcar in Berne, Switzerland. He had become very interested in the relationship between time and distance. On that day as he rode the streetcar, he said, "Suddenly, the answers flashed into my mind," and he saw a total image which "became as clear as day," and his theory of relativity came into being.

Now comes an interesting question —
Which brain gave birth to $E = mc^2$?

Because the creative brain is holistic and intuitive, one might suppose that Einstein's theory of relativity was a product of his creative brain. Surely that day in Berne, his creative brain did surge into action. But, in truth, it would be fairer to conclude his theory came from the interaction of both brains. Dr. Einstein's academic brain contained the necessary facts and figures and had posed the proper questions; his creative brain then assessed the elements and visualized the results, presenting a holistic view. Perhaps that is how significant problems are solved and the best ideas are formulated.

Utilizing the Functions of Both Brains To Improve Our Lives

How many times have you or I been faced with a problem for which we can find no solution? We analyze the elements, we sort the possibilities, but we cannot find that elusive answer. Then suddenly, while driving a car, or walking on a sidewalk, or in the midst of some unrelated activity, the solution bursts forth in our minds as if it comes from nowhere. The "nowhere" is our creative brain. Our academic brain had sorted all the elements and measured the details, but the creative brain was needed to visualize the whole and intuit a proper solution.

Our daily activities are decided by the necessity of the functions and the desires of both brains:

It is our academic brains that lead us to lectures and to watch the nightly news.

It is our creative brains that take us to the theater and to movies.

It is our academic brains that fill out our income tax forms and read for pertinent information.

It is our creative brains that urge us to pick up paint brushes and pencils for painting and drawing, and lead us to read novels, poetry and even the comic strips.

It is our academic brains that are interested in Dow Jones averages and vital statistics.

It is our creative brains that want the stereos turned on to rhythms and songs.

So when we begin to suspect that we are not one person, but two, our suspicion is probably accurate, for we are at least the result of two brains which have individual functions and desires. Our actions and schedules are the result of the interplay between these two entities. Too great an imbalance between the two may at times contribute to feelings of dissatisfaction, frustration and confusion, leading strictly academic people to be called "bookworms" and "eggheads," and the primarily creative person to be considered eccentric and unrealistic. Worst of all, if people

CLOVER
— Mary Ryan, 12

MAYBE WE WILL TOMORROW
— Tami Cottrell, 12

SPACE JOURNEY
— Frankie Franklin, 12

There is an old myth that the gifted child is a child with horn-rimmed glasses, hunchback, and with his face buried in a book. That is not true. They have a large vocabulary. They have an easy way of talking and use words accurately. They are curious, desiring to know the how's and why's of the world around them. They show an early awareness of cause and effect. They want reasons for actions and decisions. Their vocabularies are sprinkled with "Why?" and "How come?" and "Really?"

— Benjamine Fine

A real reform of the educational system will not occur until *the individual teachers learn to understand the true duality of their students' minds.* With this awareness it becomes only natural to conduct the class in a way that *keeps the attention of both the verbal and the nonverbal minds.*

The split-brain researchers have shown that one hemisphere or the other tends to dominate depending upon which one "feels more strongly" about an answer. These feelings of confidence are reinforced daily in the classroom give-and-take.

The frightening thing is that this competitive balance is so delicate. If the nonverbal mind is ignored, it pays less attention, learns less, and gradually becomes less and less able to compete. What starts out as a slight disadvantage gradually develops into a larger difference in confidence and ability. As time goes by, it becomes increasingly harder to make the nonverbal mind pay attention and participate.

To reverse this trend, teachers must become aware of the nonverbal side of each student.

— Thomas R. Blakeslee
The Right Brain

aren't given opportunities to use both brains, their potential remains untapped and much enjoyment in life is missed.

Pay Attention!

As teachers, standing before a classroom of twenty students, our challenge is not dealing with twenty brains, but forty — or forty-two if we count our own.

When we say to a class, "Pay attention," we're actually calling the academic brains of our students to order. When we see the boy or the girl in the third row begin to "drift out," or see a student dreamily staring out the window, in all probability he or she is not deliberately being inattentive, but has actually switched brains. In mathematics class or in history we can't allow that so we snap our fingers or call out the student's name, suddenly forcing him or her to switch back to the academic brain. Whether we know it or not, from the beginning of time, we human beings have been making others switch brains. If we speak to people about facts and figures, we are eliciting responses from their academic brains. If we speak in terms of schemes and dreams, or sing songs or listen to music, we are addressing their creative brains. No matter what subject we teach, we are actively urging our students to move either into the left or the right hemisphere of thinking.

If you think that having the ability to move, at will, a classroom of twenty students to use one brain or the other is exciting, then you and I are in total agreement. If we as teachers want a project which will utilize the function of each brain, independently, and the interaction of both brains to the optimum, I can think of no better project than the development and assembly of handsomely illustrated books.

To prepare such books, the students must use the functions of the academic brain for grammar, spelling, punctuation, etc., and for measuring page sizes, following sequential steps of production, properly numbering pages, learning the components of a book—text, title page, half title page, dedication, copyright, book jacket, cover, and so forth. Students must use their creative brains for subject, plot, structure, design, illustrations, etc.

As you will see, the WRITTEN & ILLUSTRATED BY...WORKSHOPS are designed to generate the maximum response from both brains. They are carefully organized to make students switch to the proper brain for each phase of development.

As a teacher, you are about to have the time of your life.

As for your students — well, they may never be the same again.

3

The Business of Creating Original Book Ideas

Forming a Publishing Company

publish:

to declare publicly, make generally known, disclose, circulate;

to place before the public;

to produce for publication or allow to be issued for distribution or sale;

to reproduce for public consumption.

LIFE OF MARAN
— Sandy Davis, 13

company:

an assemblage or association of persons or things;

an association of persons for carrying on a commercial or industrial enterprise or business.

If you want your students to develop the most creative books possible, you need to be aware of a very important key ingredient:

Tell them only what they need to know, at exactly the point when they need to know it, and nothing more!

We must be ever conscious that the academic brain loves to be presented a complete outline of step-by-step, logical procedures, so the information must be precise and to the point.

We must also remember the creative brain functions best when the framework of a new venture is not completely defined and restricted.

Therefore, we must be precise with information as to size and number of pages expected in their books and, at the same time, make sure the contents of the books are left vague enough to allow their development in imagination and creativity.

To maintain this essential balance is a rather neat trick, but happily, it is an attainable and simple one to perform. Although it may require some adjustment in our thinking processes as teachers, anyone can do it. In the course of these pages, I will not only tell you how to do it, I will also offer many of the reasons why. As you will see, the Workshop will be segmented by sessions outlined in very complete lesson plans. By following the proposed key ingredient, I will **tell you what you need to know, at exactly the point you need to know it.**

How To Announce to Students They Will Write and Illustrate Books

The announcement should be simple and direct. And the timing is important. If I had my druthers, I would hope you pick a time which would not allow any discussion. For example, if you plan to begin the project on a Monday, then on the Friday before — one minute before the bell rings — call the class to order and say with no uncertain determination:

"On Monday, we are starting a very exciting project. Each and every

THE FOUR WILD HORSES
— Cara Anne Caputo, 10

MARIA
— Laura Tucker, 13

Creativity was in each of us as a small child. Among adults it is almost nonexistent. The question is, what has happened to this enormous and universal human resource? The answer is that our colossal system of education is concerned mainly with acquiring a body of knowledge, memorizing of facts, and finding answers to problems, all of which are already known to someone else, rather than with creativity.

— Harold H. Anderson
Michigan State University

THE FRIENDLY VISITORS
— Ryan Williams, 11

one of you will begin writing and illustrating a book of your own. I think you'll enjoy it."

The bell rings.

Perfect!

You have just given them information which is precise and direct. Their academic brains have been only slightly threatened. If they have time for asking any questions, their questions will come from their academic brains:

"What do we have to write about?"

"How many pages will our books have?"

"Will you count off for spelling?"

And so on.

If any of the students try to press for answers, just tell them they'll be told everything they need to know on Monday, then change the subject or shoo them on their way.

In that simple announcement (and this is the fun part) you made direct contact with not only their academic brains, but you have also alerted their creative brains.

In each head, the creative brain begins to wonder —

"If this isn't another report, what is it? Maybe this will be **my** chance. A book! Perhaps I will get to write a book! And illustrations too! How about that! I wonder if it can be funny? How about an adventure story — with lots of blood and gore? Or a fairytale? Or maybe it could be about a journey into outerspace or about some trouble in a family, or . . . ?"

These reactions are exactly what you want. And if you say nothing more, it is exactly what you'll get.

Over the weekend, the students will have two days to consider the idea in a nonactive manner. The academic brain hasn't been given enough information to form a tangible format and cannot begin to outline or plan. So the creative brain is free to imagine and is allowed to bounce one idea after another from brain cell to brain cell. The creative brain also has the opportunity to observe the activities of the weekend from a new perspective — from that of a writer in search of a story. It will become more aware of conversations it hears, television it watches, books it reads, etc.

When I know I'm about to begin a new book, I am always amazed by the enormous amounts of information that I absorb in my normal course of events without my actively seeking them. Things that would otherwise go unnoticed take on keener meaning, offering unlimited ideas and possibilities.

You have just announced the students will write and illustrate a book. That's a new idea! Now that idea will be set into motion within their daily lives and their creative brains will begin to sort information which will allow that idea to grow and take shape. It is not an aggressive act, but it is performed by an automatic system. It is a time of free thinking that requires no planned action and no outlay of energy. It just happens. It's rather amazing how our brains work.

Making Contact with the Creative Brain

To offer your students' creative brains the best opportunities to become active, we must scramble the thinking processes in their academic brains or at least keep them unsettled during the initial phases of book development.

During the first session of the WRITTEN & ILLUSTRATED

BY...WORKSHOP, I present a thirty-five minute audio/visual program which offers synopses of my twenty-three published books and shows the students more than three hundred illustrations, including pencil drawings, pen and ink, full-color and so forth.

I began showing the program in the first Workshop, not because it would provide any flash of insight into how the creative brain works, but to save time. I realized if I didn't tell students about my work in an organized way, I would constantly be answering questions about my work when I should be giving them information they need to create their books. Since I am both a writer and illustrator and since I have experimented in a wide variety of genres — novels, biographies, self-help books, adult and juvenile fiction, poetry and so forth — the program also reveals to students that I like all kinds of books and I am interested in many subjects. Because I have demonstrated I am open and receptive to a wide variety of subjects, students now feel safe in developing any type of book they wish. To offer students such creative freedom is very important.

Margo Rommel, 12

This Is My Favorite Book

If I could not use my own books as examples, I would offer a list of my favorite books to achieve the same results, and I advise you to use the following procedure, which was tested by teachers and found to be most successful:

Go to the public library or to your own bookcase and select twenty books that are very different from each other in subject and genre. This should only take a few minutes.

Before class, stack the books on the chair behind your desk or on a shelf nearby. When the class is assembled, select one book and hold it up. Simply announce the title and the author and offer a very quick synopsis.

For instance, say:

> *A TALE OF TWO CITIES, by Charles Dickens, tells of the political struggle during the French Revolution and of human courage during a time of war. The characters are so clearly drawn and offer insight into the personal reactions that the book is as valid today as when it was written.*

And then you say the very important line:

> *This is my favorite book.*

Stand the book upright on your desk. Then pick up the second book, offer the title, name of author and a quick synopsis.

Then conclude:

> *This is my favorite book.*

Go through the whole stack one by one. Obviously, the class will begin to react to the last line with chuckles and will begin to anticipate your

SUGGESTED LESSON PLAN

Teacher Preparation:

Select your list of favorite books and bring them to class.

Have brief synopsis in mind for each one.

Review Session 1 in book.

Materials Needed:

The Twenty Books.

Activities:

Show each book and give synopsis ending each with—
"This is my favorite book."

After your list is presented you may have students tell titles of some of their favorite books.

Time Required:

45 minutes

Assignment:

None

EAT THE MOUSE, CAT!
— April Clore, 11

concluding remark for each book. When you finish, there should be at least twenty books standing upright on your desk and you should tell them your desktop is not large enough to hold all your favorite books, because the list could very well go into the hundreds. And if you like, you might mention a few other choices.

Then you might have each student give the title of at least one favorite book and a brief synopsis. No matter what title a student offers, you MUST show enthusiasm or at least say, "That sounds interesting," even if one student selects the *ANNUAL COLLECTION OF MAD MAGAZINE*. Today, you like everything! That throws them off guard.

Bring the session to a close and get them up and out of the room. If you are a secondary teacher, the bell will signal the end of class. If you are an elementary school teacher, move them out to recess or to lunch. Either way, get them out of the room so they can move about for at least ten minutes.

SESSION 2

SUGGESTED LESSON PLAN

Teacher Preparation:

Make copies of Job Application.
Make copies of Contract.
Review Session 2 in book.

Materials Needed:

1 Job Application per student.
2 copies of Contract per student.

Activities:

Repeat Announcement.
Vote on class or publishing company.
Fill out Job Applications.
Fill out and sign Contracts.
Students begin to write.

Time Required:

45 minutes

Assignment:

None

How To Form a Publishing Company

Begin the session by repeating the announcement you previously made.

"During the next two weeks (three if you choose), each one of you will write and illustrate a complete book."

Allow no time for discussion.

You have just made an assignment. It is not negotiable.

Now tell the class in order to get the project started, a decision must be reached. They are allowed to choose between:

One: Their books may be developed in a classroom setting. You will be the teacher and they will be students; or

Two: The group can form a publishing company. Without discussion, instruct them to vote on the following:

How many want a class?

How many prefer a publishing company?

I promise you the publishing company will win hands down. Or I suppose in this case with hands up.

Now the publishing company must become a real entity. Have the students suggest names and vote. You need not allow much time for discussion. When three or four names are suggested, call for a vote.

Once you have the name of the publishing company, tell them, "As President of the (So-and-So) Publishing Company (yes, you are automatically the president, not by vote but by your decree), "I'll need editors and art directors." So students will need to fill out Applications for these positions. Pass out the Xeroxed copies of the form which is printed on the facing page.

APPLICATION FOR EMPLOYMENT

DATE:_____

NAME:_____

ADDRESS:_____
                        (street)

_____
                        (city)

_____
(state)   (zip code)

TELEPHONE NUMBER:_____

PHOTO
OF
APPLICANT

AGE:_____

I WISH TO SECURE EMPLOYMENT AS AN EDITOR AND ART DIRECTOR AT THE:

_____

QUALIFICATIONS:_____

_____

_____

_____

EXPERIENCE:_____

_____

_____

_____

SPECIAL INTERESTS AND HOBBIES:_____

_____

I WISH TO SECURE THESE JOBS BECAUSE:_____

_____

_____

_____

_____
(Signature of Applicant)

PERICLA
— Beatriz Carrancedo, 10

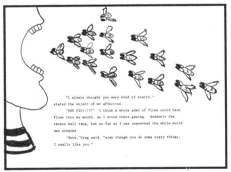

CHERISHED MEMORIES
— Michelle Mettlach, 12

WHY ME?
— Barbara Tirre Noble

Jennifer Furey, 13

Application for Employment

Have students fill out the necessary information: NAME, ADDRESS, TELEPHONE NUMBER and AGE.

I WISH TO SECURE EMPLOYMENT AS AN EDITOR AND ART DIRECTOR AT THE ———————————————————— .

Have them write in the name of the publishing company they have chosen.

Then discuss each section of the Application with them.

QUALIFICATIONS:

Each student has wonderful qualifications. They are more important than students might suppose.

"I am alive" — that's certainly an important qualification.

"I have lived for ————— years." So they have experiences.

"I can read."

"I can write."

"I have seen pictures."

"I have read books."

"I can draw pictures."

"I have seen dramas on television and in the movies."

"I have seen stage plays."

"I can spell," and so on.

— all excellent qualifications.

EXPERIENCE:

They probably have more experience than they realize.

"I have lived three years in Paris, France."

"I have lived my entire life on a farm."

   —"or in a big city," "or in a small community."

"I have lived with a family so I know about family life."

"I have friends so I know about associations with people."

"I don't get along with everyone so I know about conflicts."

"I have gone to school so I know about rules."

"I have flown in an airplane."

"I have been in Washington, D.C. and a number of states."

Or, "I've never been more than 100 miles from home."

All of these experiences are important, which may surprise students. Either individually or collectively, these experiences offer them valuable resources of information.

For instance, I have never lived on a farm. If I were going to write a book which takes place on a farm, I would have to spend time researching farm life and procedures before I could begin such a book. Yet any third-grade student who has lived on a farm already has such information. His or her knowledge about farm life is far superior to mine.

SPECIAL INTERESTS AND HOBBIES:

Have students list the things they like to do — skating, skiing, camping, building model airplanes, sewing, cooking, watching television, reading books, going to movies, fishing, playing video games, playing chess — whatever.

I WISH TO SECURE THESE JOBS BECAUSE:

Any reasons students offer are acceptable.

"I love books." (That's a splendid one!)

"I am told I have to." (So what, you and I are told we have to do many things we are not eager to attempt.)

"The pay is good." — I love this one. (How little they know.)

Then be sure they sign the Applications.

Instruct students to bring in a picture the following day or, if you choose, tell them you'll bring in a Polaroid camera and take their pictures at a later time. Be sure by the end of the week a picture is attached to each Application, which certainly makes it complete.

Now, collect the Applications and welcome your students to the company.

The act of filling out the Application forms is by no means busywork. It serves some extremely important functions for students:

- It allows them to review their lives from past to present.
- It gives them the opportunity to list many of the positive attributes they possess which will prove valuable in developing books.
- It strengthens the concept of forming a real company.
- It begins to prepare them for work situations they will experience as adults.

When I first started teaching professional writing courses, I had the participants write an autobiography as the first assignment for the reasons we've just discussed, and because I felt it was very important for me as a teacher to become aware of how very interesting my students are as people and become aware of the experiences from which they may draw.

I always read the autobiographies very carefully and often reviewed them as I read the creative efforts of the students.

Filling out and collecting the Applications should not take more than twenty minutes at most. Now you are ready for one of the most important steps in the creation of a book.

SUPER FATS
— Tony Rennick, 14

DRAGON OF ORD
— David McAdoo, 10

A Contract of Agreement:

Pass out one Contract to each student.

Instruct the students to write in the date on the Contract.

Have them write their names after AUTHOR/ILLUSTRATOR.

The name of the publishing company they have selected comes after PUBLISHER.

Have them stop at that point.

Before they write any more, it is important the Contract is read in full and they understand every line. It is so important that you should read all sections aloud to them.

When you get to the line that says, NUMBER OF PAGES, instruct them to write in "16."

Tell them these pages are the text of the book. They will include the story and illustrations, but will not include the opening pages (title pages, half title, and so forth) or the closing page.

After you read MEDIA SELECTED FOR ILLUSTRATION, tell them not to write anything down at this point, but discuss types of media they might choose to use — pencil, water color, pen and ink, tempera, felt tips. But **not** chalk nor crayons. Chalk smears. Crayons are extremely difficult to use in preparing quality illustrations. (I can't understand how first and second graders use crayons so successfully.) And in an assembled book, crayon and chalk will rub off on the opposing pages.

Then read the rest of the Contract to them. If they have any questions

contract:

an agreement between two or more persons or parties to do or not to do something.

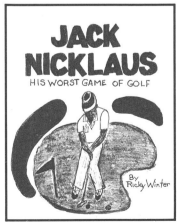

Ricky Winter, 14

CONTRACT OF AGREEMENT

PARTIES OF AGREEMENT: DATE _____

    1. AUTHOR/ILLUSTRATOR: _____

    2. PUBLISHER: _____

IT IS MUTUALLY AGREED: AUTHOR/ILLUSTRATOR will write an original book of superior quality and prepare the most brilliant illustrations for said book within a period of time not to exceed _____ working days and nights. Within the framework of this time allowed, AUTHOR/ILLUSTRATOR will assemble said book, design a masterpiece book jacket and bind all materials with the express purpose of delighting and astounding all readers and viewers of said book.

PROPOSED BOOK TITLE: _____

BRIEF SYNOPSIS OF STORY: _____

_____

_____

_____

_____

_____

NUMBER OF PAGES: _____   MEDIA FOR ILLUSTRATIONS: _____

AUTHOR/ILLUSTRATOR hereby promises to explore and expand the widest boundaries of his or her creative potentials; to pay the utmost attention to all instructions; and to be keenly aware and appreciative of the creations of other authors and illustrators for the duration of and beyond the time limits of this specific Contract of Agreement.

PUBLISHER also promises to recognize and delight in the creative genius of AUTHOR/ILLUSTRATOR; to promote the development of professional attitudes and discipline; to encourage the growth and acceleration of imagination and skills; and to express both respect and delight by the marvelous elements within and the outstanding results of AUTHOR/ILLUSTRATOR'S said book.

_____

AUTHOR/ILLUSTRATOR

_____

PRESIDENT OF PUBLISHING COMPANY

about what is written in the Contract you may answer them. But do not, I repeat, do not, discuss any book ideas with them.

Now you come to the most important step in pulling from them the most creative ideas for books.

Tell them they have **five minutes** to write a brief synopsis of their proposed books, to write in their titles, and to designate what media will be used for the illustrations in the spaces allowed.

Allow no time for discussion. Start timing.

Now apply the pressure.

At the end of one minute, announce **four minutes** are remaining.

At the end of two minutes, announce only **three minutes** are left, and so on.

At the end of five minutes, tell them to **stop.**

Then to prove that you are a considerate person, ask if anyone needs more time. If they are all completed, then go to the next step. But if even one student needs more time, be generous and give only one additional minute for him or her to finish and the others to review their work.

At minute's end, pass out a second copy of the Contract and instruct them to duplicate the same information on the second copy. Allow them five minutes to do so, which is more than enough time.

Instruct your students to sign both copies of their Contracts and to bring them to your desk, one by one. You glance over their titles and synopses and say to the effect, "Oh, that looks like a terrific idea. I'm really eager to see your finished book."

You sign one copy of the Contract and hand it back to the student, then sign the other one and retain it for your file.

As soon as you have signed the Contract, tell the student to return to his or her desk and start writing. Then look over the next person's Contract.

It is terribly important that the students commence writing immediately. If the building catches on fire, rush them to the nearest exit with pencil and paper in hand and, as soon as you are outside, guide them to a safe distance and have them sit down and WRITE.

Give the Creative Brain Its Chance To Create

To get the most creative book ideas out of the students, this type of deadline pressure is extremely important. Follow it to the letter. Under such time pressure, the academic brains of your students will quickly relinquish command. Remember the academic brain likes to perform in a step-by-step procedure and loves to have the time to analyze every phase of a project before committing itself. Under the pressure of time, the academic brain will gladly step aside, and the creative brain will almost cheer for now is its chance! The creative brain loves ideas and holistic approaches — it is ready to intuit and visualize concepts without demanding precise detail. It has just been given the opportunity to decide on the subject of the book, the title, and what media to use for illustrations.

The younger the students, the easier they will handle the pressure of time, for their decisions are quickly made. If you want to see people "climb the walls and attempt the ceilings," you should observe adults who participate in my Workshops. When I announce they have only five minutes to make such decisions, they are literally thrown into a panic. After they finish filling out their Contracts, they often sit in a state of

THE TIGER THAT RAN OUT OF THE ZOO
— Chip Myers, 7

BETSY'S REVENGE
— Andrea Steiner, 14

I'M IN THE MIDDLE (AND I HATE IT)
— Ken Trantham, 12

ROCKVILLE—THE CITY OF FLOWERS
— Yael Joseph

CAT TAILS
—Mark Brandau, 12

TO FLY AS THE EAGLE
— Larry West

TEDDY THE DISSATISFIED JELLY
BEAN — Emily Arthur, 10

confusion. Many of them will come up to me later and say, "I made a terrible mistake on my Contract."

"What is that?" I ask.

"Well," they admit, "even though you warned us not to decide on a subject until this morning, I already decided what kind of book I would do."

"Oh, that's alright," I reply. "So what's the problem?"

"Well, I don't understand it," they say. "That's not the book I wrote down on the Contract. I wrote another idea instead."

I know full well they are about to ask if they can backtrack and write the original, well-organized, but stale idea they had brought with them. But I cut them off at the pass.

"Oh, I'm sure this new idea is a much better one," I tell them and walk away.

And in truth, I'm sure it is. Without knowing it, they had just received vital messages from their creative brains, forcing their academic brains to adjust and yield to such decisions which will provide them with much more exciting experiences.

Don't be surprised if several of your students tell you the same thing. When they do, just smile at them reassuringly and tell them you're positive it is for the best. Then you turn and walk away.

Do All the Stories Have To Be 16 Pages?

That's bound to be the first question students will ask.

The answer is Yes. However, and this is very important, these sixteen pages may be divided by text and illustrations in any way students choose.

"But how long do the stories have to be?" they will want to know.

Tell them: "As long as you decide they should be. Eight of the sixteen pages may be full text with eight pages of illustrations. Or each page may have only one paragraph of text with full-page illustrations." (Examples in outer column)

If you want your students to develop their most creative books, you do not want to set minimums or maximums for the amount of text they must write. You should only tell them the number of pages they are to use in expressing the total idea and leave the number of words and the sizes of illustrations to their imaginations. Allow their creative brains to make these decisions.

What may surprise you (and your students too) is that students, who usually write the least amount of words for an assignment, will find themselves writing pages and pages on their own. You may also discover some students, who normally write lengthly pieces of prose, will now write brief stories and experiment with large illustrations. Of course, this is what makes the Workshop so exciting for both you and your students. You have no idea what will burst forth from your students' creative brains, but as soon as you offer input of information into those brains, you must allow their choice of output of product.

At most, they probably have no more than fifteen to twenty minutes to write before the second session draws to a close. In the last minute or two of the session, tell them you wish to make an assignment for the evening and they are to follow your instructions precisely. Until you meet for the following session, they are not to do **any** work on their books. Tell them to do whatever homework they may have from other classes, but to enjoy a relaxing evening, reading a book or watching television or whatever they choose. That will really throw them for a loop. They will either think you have some diabolical scheme in mind or you've really "lost your marbles."

What About Amendments to the Contracts?

Should we allow the writers to change their titles or their stories during the course of the Workshop? Why not? As a professional writer, I have the privilege to change a title up to press time. I think my students deserve the same courtesy. As they become more familiar with their books, they may think of more appropriate titles or discover a better story. If they do, have them note the new title or change of plot on both Contract copies, with both of you initialing the alteration to make it official. Your students have just learned something else — how contracts are amended.

I allow students to change titles at any time — until the very last — but I will only allow them to embark on a new story prior to the deadline of the first draft.

Leave Their Titles Alone and They Will Come Home — Splendidly!

You might have noticed that before you had students fill out their Contracts (which required their composing titles for their books) there was no mention of the necessary ingredients that constitute good titles.

This was not an oversight on my part.

In the first Workshop I conducted, before the students filled out their Contracts, I forgot to refer to my notes and failed to discuss titles with them. It really upset me because I had developed a beautiful presentation about the importance of title development, stressing how very difficult it is to come up with exactly the appropriate title for a book.

When I arrived home that night I was very annoyed with myself, certain I had hindered the preparation of all the students' books. I pulled their Contracts out of my briefcase and quickly reviewed the titles, among which were the following:

JUNIOR GENIUS

MEPHISTOPHILES

WHEN MIDNIGHT COMES

BENJAMIN GOES AWAY

ALMOST A LIFETIME

RUNAWAY

THE ADVENTURES OF
SIR SCOOPINPOOP

THE CONFLICTING POWER

MAYBE WE WILL TOMORROW

AGE OF AQUARIUS

and so forth.

I was astounded. There wasn't one bad title in the whole group. All of the students knew how to write titles. Or at least their creative brains knew the secret — whatever. They certainly had experienced enough titular input from books they had read and from movies and television they had seen.

On the chance that I had a weird group on my first outing, I carried the materials for the Book Title Development presentation with me to the next two Workshops, but never used them.

STOP THE WORLD, I WANT TO GET OFF — Laurel L. Powell, 12

THE DAY FOUR DOGS DIED — Charles Baker

Dax Gay, 12

Clint Kajinami, 12

THE DRAGON AND SIR SCOOPINPOOP
—Daniel Childress, 17

CAMP NAZARETH
— Marsha Walsh

Although adults seem to have more difficulty in writing titles than do younger students, all of them eventually come up with super titles. And I may not be the brightest guy on the block, but I do know enough to leave well enough alone. I would advise you to do the same.

The Sweet Smell of Success

If you are teaching in an elementary school, you have more control over their next activity. Get them up and out of the room. Now would be a perfect time for music or recess or lunch or even an art class. You have placed them under enough pressure so let them relax. If you are in secondary school with your class moving on to a math or history class, all you can do is pity the next teacher. She's got to attempt to switch their complete attention to the academic brain.

You have now directed your students through two hours of the Workshop. In these short periods of time, you have shown them you like all kinds of books and are receptive to their ideas. Together, you have formed and named a publishing company. You have been made president — perhaps by some sleight of hand on your part, but I'm sure many have used more devious means to become head of a large or even small corporation. Just consider that your company is about to produce twenty to thirty new books within the next two or three weeks. You understand, of course, even the largest publishers don't produce so many titles in such a short period of time.

You now have Applications for enough editors and art directors to insure the success of the book production.

You have Contracts with a stable of authors and illustrators.

And within the course of only two hours, your authors are already writing their books.

As the presidential head of your company, you've just earned a four-star rating. Congratulations!

Expect Immediate Improvements

When you begin such a course with your students, expect improvement.

When I taught my first writing class, I made an ignorant mistake.

I was too cautious. I told students not to expect major improvements or miracles in their initial assignments.

Most of my students heard me and they believed me, so they didn't make immediate improvements. But have you ever noticed that all students don't listen to everything you say?

Three of my students either didn't hear my warning or didn't believe me or didn't care, and in defiance made immediate improvements in their writing.

When they told me and the class of their outstanding breakthroughs, I was highly suspect, especially when, during the following session, other students became just as excited about the improvements in their writing.

Although I remained a reluctant doubting Thomas through several more assignments, I finally confessed to the students I had made a mistake. I told them they not only **should** expect but **could** expect immediate improvement with each and every assignment.

Tell your students you expect rapid improvements in their writing and illustrating skills and they should be just as optimistic. Improvements will be forthcoming.

Kelly Johnston, 13

The Mysterious Red Balloon
Written & Illustrated By Kelly Johnston

How To Conquer the Power of the White

The Writing Begins

HELP, I'M A SLAVE
— Paige Mistler, 12

THE CAR THAT ATE CHEESE
— Harry McKinney, 10

It is extremely important that we set up the proper atmosphere in which students can easily and joyfully create.

If we tell students that writing is extremely difficult, most of them will soon agree. Only a very timid or courageous few will defy such warnings and go on to write their poetry in the safety of their rooms at night, or continue to write short stories and articles for the school newspaper. It is easy to dissuade most people from writing, but it's a shallow and hollow victory.

The truth is, writing is not difficult — it is easy! Spelling may be difficult. The use of proper grammar and punctuation may be difficult. But writing stories and expressing oneself in the written word is not only easy, it can be fun and even exhilarating.

When I first began teaching professional writing courses, some colleagues warned me that I would be lucky if I could find one person out of thirty who could write a decent piece of prose. So I prepared for the worst. I could never have guessed what a surprise awaited me. I soon discovered that not only could all thirty students write "decent" prose, but most of them, in a very short period of time, could write exciting and inventive stories.

All Positives — No Negatives

After I read and edit their work, I find it very easy to review a student's work, face-to-face. As a matter of fact, it is a joyous experience because I never write a negative comment on anyone's work. I believe my function as a teacher is to improve the work, not destroy the person. Negatives are destructive to the creative spirit. If my comments are positive and the editing improves the work, the students are always open to suggestions and, even better, they appreciate my assistance.

In the next chapter, we will discuss the role of the editor and the process of editing.

MY LIFE
—Vickki Barnes, 6

CHESTER
—Kari McKenzie, 15

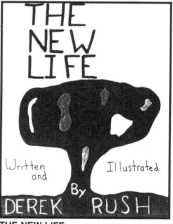

THE NEW LIFE
— Derek Rush, 11

I never begin a seminar or Workshop without a total and complete conviction that everyone in the group has the spark of creative genius. And time and again, my students' work substantiates my conviction. I am convinced my students do not achieve and excel because I am such a good teacher. My students produce because the spark of creativity within them stirs when I give them the opportunity, encouragement and freedom to express themselves.

Students also learn a great deal from each other. The younger ones tend to work very directly and decisively, without nearly as much concern about what others think of their work. By mid-week, the younger students are always way ahead in developing their books, which influences the older ones to throw caution aside and get on with it. However, the older ones, through experience, know how to schedule their time and energies to complete the work. So the younger ones learn much in this regard by observing their older counterparts.

If your class is composed of students who are in the same age group, no matter. You still share many of these same advantages because, more than likely, you have students who work on many levels of skill in both writing and illustrating, giving everyone the opportunity and fun of learning from each other.

Clearing the Field — Eliminating Barriers

In teaching writing, I long ago concluded if people have some basic skills in writing a language, most of them could be writing professional materials in a very short period of time. The difference between writing a simple letter to a friend or relative and writing a magazine article or book is a very thin margin, mostly concerning the organization of thoughts and length of the final product.

There are only six reasons for people not to write publishable materials, and lack of time is **not** one of them. I know of no author who, in the beginning of his or her career, had the time to write. They somehow made the time. They stayed up nights or even better arose earlier in the mornings. They stole time from their paying jobs and squeezed precious time from their association with relatives and friends.

The six reasons why people do not write are:

1. **They have no quarantee of readers.**
   A big deterrent. How can we be expected to even write a letter if we have no one to whom we can write?

2. **They have no deadlines.**
   No one is breathing down their necks or threatening to cancel payment, so there is no financial urgency.

3. **They don't have an editor.**
   Without someone to earnestly check the spelling and punctuation and flow of context, it is terribly difficult to face blank pages, day after day.

4. **They don't know how to edit their own work.**
   Every line that is written can't be considered as precious and inexpendable. The flow of the work must be tightened, embellished and polished.

5. They don't write often enough.

Writing is like riding a bicycle — the more you do it, the more proficient you, the writer, become.

6. They have too little or no regard for the reader.

I think this last reason is the one that separates nonpublishable material from publishable material. The beginning writer concentrates too much on the writing and neglects to consider how the material is going to be read.

During the course, students will be:
  provided readers;
  given deadlines;
  assigned editors;
  taught how to edit; and
  offered opportunities to write often enough
  to complete an end product.

And as for time — well, they will soon be scheduling their time — not because we threaten them with grades, but because their work will become more meaningful to them. After all, they are in the process of writing and illustrating a book — a real book! It is not a mere assignment that only the teacher will read and grade. It will be a tangible product they can hold in their hands and one that many people will take pleasure in reading. It is a thing of here and now. It is theirs — a very important incentive to creativity!

A Real Product!

I have always felt in teaching writing that journalism teachers have certain advantages over English teachers. News reporting has a definite style, stressing the "five *Ws*" and the "one *H*" — *who, what, when, where, why* and *how*. Also in news articles, the synopsis of the whole story is told in the first paragraph and the succeeding paragraphs offer added details, going from the most important to the least important.

But the main incentive journalism teachers can offer is the immediacy of the product — something is going to happen with the article — it is going to be **printed**! Other people are going to read what the writer has written. Whether good or bad or in-between, as soon as that newspaper is printed, it is seen by others and the writer gets an immediate feedback. If the writer is lucky and has done a good job, he or she will receive words of praise and congratulations. If not, he or she can expect the "slings and arrows of outrageous" readers.

Because the book is a product, you will have some students who have never before shown outstanding or even average abilities, suddenly grab hold of the ideas and blossom before your eyes. I have at least one of these children in every Workshop. He or she doesn't do particularly well in school, rather drifts from one class to another, is barely noticed and usually forgotten or easily ignored.

Sometimes these children surprise us after their graduation from school. One day we just happen to hear these do-nothings in school have formed their own companies and are on the way to being millionaires. We can't believe it. But what we have overlooked is the fact that these children

CURIOUS GEORGE GETS ICED
— Warren Tandoc, 13

THE DRAGON OF ORD
— David McAdoo, 10

FRIENDS
— Beth Arthur

happen to be product-oriented and schools are not normally product-oriented institutions.

You should hope and pray you have such children in your groups. As they astound you and their parents with their finished products, they will make you look like the greatest teacher since Socrates. More importantly, you may have provided such children with their first opportunities to create in an atmosphere that intrigues them.

SESSION 3

SUGGESTED LESSON PLAN

Teacher Preparation:

Make list of Editor and Art Director assignments.

Reread all of Session 3.

Materials Needed:

None

Activities:

Review list of Editor and Art Director assignments.

Present basic elements of a story.

Read *Three Little Pigs* aloud to group.

Discuss the "Power of the White."

Read aloud section from RALPH MILLER.

Instruct students to begin writing.

Time Required:

45 minutes

Assignment:

None

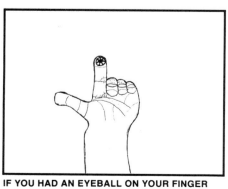

IF YOU HAD AN EYEBALL ON YOUR FINGER
— Terrilyn McCormick, 11

Teacher's Preparation for the Third Session

Before conducting the third session of your WRITTEN & ILLUSTRATED BY...WORKSHOP, as President of the So-and-So Publishing Company, you should take the time to assign each student as an editor for another student and each student as an art director for yet another student. During the course of developing the book, each student will work very directly with four other students — each person becoming an editor for one writer and an art director for still another. Each will have a different person as editor for his or her own book and should have a fourth person who functions as an art director for his or her book.

The key to success is to mix the people more than match them. Place people with lesser skills with those who have better skills. Break up groups of close friends and buddies. What you purposely want to do is scramble the class as much as possible so each person is working with people who he or she does not usually work. Such an approach will alter the dynamics of the class and place the structure of the academic brain in a state of flux, which is exactly what you want to achieve.

Since you may know your students, you have an advantage over the way I have to assign editors and art directors. If you don't know your students well, then you might want to adopt one of my methods:

Have the students pass their Contracts to the person who is sitting directly behind them, bringing the Contract from the back row to the head of the front row. The people who now hold the Contracts write their names on the line designated "Editor."

Now repeat the procedure. Everyone passes the Contract they have just signed to the person sitting directly behind them, bringing the Contracts from the back row to the front. Now have the students sign their names after "Art Director" on the Contract they presently hold.

Collect all the Contracts and make a master list designating each person who has been assigned as an editor or art director with the respective author's name. Be sure you keep a copy of the master list. Post a copy on the wall for the duration of the publishing process, making sure each student has copied down his or her job assignments of editor and art director.

Now you are ready to present the next piece of information your writers will need.

The Basic Elements of a Story

Tell your students you are about to present a college course in the basic elements of a story within the next ten minutes.

Inform them every good story contains THREE basic elements. Ask your students what they think these basic elements are. Consider and discuss their answers.

The words you are looking for are:

BEGINNING — every good story needs a beginning.

Once you have settled on the first basic element, the next two become obvious — a MIDDLE and an END. Write these on the chalkboard:

BEGINNING
MIDDLE
END

What should a good **beginning** present?

A good beginning should present setting and characters.

If the story is to be interesting, what does the **middle** need?

An interesting story must have **a conflict** or **a problem.**

What needs to happen before the **end**?

A **solution** must be found for the **problem.**

Or the **conflict** must be resolved.

Simple, simple, simple.

There are two other ingredients for every good story: Whether the story is a tragedy or a comedy, it should contain elements of **humor** and elements of **seriousness**.

All the classic comedies have their serious moments. Shakespeare, Charlie Chaplin and Neil Simon have certainly displayed their understanding of that.

And all serious stories are enhanced if they contain moments of humor. Shakespeare definitely knew this. Although both HAMLET and MACBETH are tragedies, they contain some very funny lines and humorous situations within their plots.

Now offer a story as an example. It should be a story that everyone already knows and as much **below** their grade level as possible. You may use any story you wish. I usually tell them the story of THE THREE LITTLE PIGS. You may read the following aloud if you wish:

DOO-DAD THE KATYDID
— Ronda Freese

THE PIG WITH THE BLUE NOSE
— Stephen Patton

THE THREE LITTLE PIGS

Once upon a time, there were three little pigs who said goodbye to their mother and left their home to seek their fortunes.

The first little pig was a lazy little pig, so he built his house with straw.

The second little pig didn't like to work either, so he built his house of sticks.

See, everyone knows the story.

But the third little pig was an industrious little pig, and he planned for the future by building his house of brick.

In the woods nearby, there lived a big bad wolf.

One day the wolf came out of the woods and walked up to the first little pig's house of straw, and said,

"Little pig, little pig, let me come in!"

But the little pig answered, "Not by the hair of my chinny-chin-chin!"

"Then I'll huff and I'll puff and I'll blow your house in!" said the big bad wolf. And he huffed and he puffed and he huffed and he puffed and he blew the house in.

It should be noted, at this point, that there is a variation in the story. If you grew up in the United States, most likely you were told that the straw house collapsed and the first little pig ran to the stick house of the second little pig. But in Europe, fairytales are taken more seriously and, should you have lived there, you would have been told that after the wolf blew the house down, he ate the little pig, which is surely a more serious version — especially for the pig. For the writer of the story it also simplifies things in that there is now one less character with which to deal.

Then the wolf came to the stick house of the second little pig and said, "Little pig, little pig, let me come in!"
"Not by the hair of my chinny-chin-chin!"

Obviously the same dialogue as in the previous scene, but it is quite effective and, since all the lines rhyme, they are easy to remember.

"Then I'll huff and I'll puff and I'll blow your house in!"

Again, you have the choice between the American or the European version, yet eliminating another character or having the first little pig and the second little pig run to their brother's brick house.

When the wolf arrived at the brick house of the third little pig, he said, "Little pig, little pig, let me come in!"
"Not by the hair of my chinny-chin-chin!"
So he huffed and he puffed and he huffed and he puffed, but he could not blow the house down.

Whereupon the clever wolf climbed up on the roof and decided to go down the chimney.

I mean, after all, lunch was waiting inside and if we're telling the American version of the story, the wolf by now is famished.

But the third little pig (*remember we already decided that he was the industrious one*) had a pot of scalding hot water steaming over the fire in the fireplace, and when the wolf dropped down the chimney, boy was he surprised!

Now we have another choice of the European or American version. In the European version, the wolf is boiled to death, which I suppose is poetic justice after murdering the first and second little pigs. Instead, the socially acceptable American version espouses prevention of cruelty to animals by having the wolf hit the water and, faster than Saint Nick, scale the chimney and run off into the woods never to be seen again. In the classic Disney film, the little pigs join hooves and dance around in a circle, singing, "Who's afraid of the big bad wolf?" which some thirty years later provided Barbra Streisand with a hit recording.

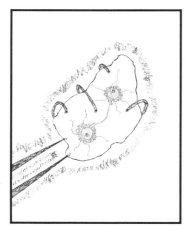

SURVIVING LATTICE
— Brian Clark, 13

DAY OF DOOM TURNS TO DELIGHT
— Deanna Purcell, 12

The story of the three little pigs certainly has all the basic elements of a good story.

In the **beginning**, the characters are easily introduced and defined. We know the good guys from the bad guy, and the one of high moral and industrial attributes from the shiftless wastrels and the villain.

The **setting** is anywhere, but since the three leading characters are pigs, a rural locale is implied, especially since the Pig brothers don't have to go through the red tape required to obtain a building permit. Besides, we know that pigs do not live in cities. However, I have no doubt I saw two the last time I rode a subway in New York City.

Be that as it may, the **conflict** or the **problem** begins when the entrance of the big bad wolf causes the opposing wills of the characters to be brought into action. The wolf is hungry and he wants a good meal. The pigs do not wish to comply by becoming his meal.

Once the wolf is either rendered into lard or runs away yelping into the woods, the **conflict** is resolved and the story is concluded — *the end.*

The story also has the other two basic ingredients. There is an element of **seriousness** which has to do with hunger and survival. And there is also **humor** injected. I defy anyone to say, "Not by the hair of my chinny-chin-chin," without at least smiling.

As you read or tell this fascinating story to your students, all the points are covered and made.

There is one type of story that defies this pattern — *the mystery.*

A good mystery does not start at the **beginning** — it usually starts in the **middle.** Who placed the icepick in the beautiful blonde? The story searches for "whodunit." Once the **beginning** is found, the culprit is caught. We have the **end.**

Now then, I assure you that in ten minutes we have had a full college course in structure and plot development. I know, because I had the course. All I have done is eliminate hours of tedious boredom and useless talk, which have very little to do with the process of creative writing.

The Right Approach To Writing

There's only one way I know to start writing — you start writing. One has to have either the audacity or the courage to attack the most formidable foe — the blank sheet of paper. If one is going to write or draw or paint, no matter, he or she must CONQUER THE POWER OF THE WHITE.

In my book, THE ONE AND ONLY SECOND AUTOBIOGRAPHY OF RALPH MILLER — THE DOG WHO KNEW HE WAS A BOY, the central character, Ralph, has decided to write a book and is faced with the same dilemma all writers must overcome. He decides to phone an author who lives nearby for advice — Yours Truly. You may either read the following scene aloud to your class in total or, if you prefer, tell the class in your own words how Winston Churchill learned to conquer the power of the white.

Mr. Miller writes:

THE ONE AND ONLY SECOND AUTOBIOGRAPHY OF RALPH MILLER—THE DOG WHO KNEW HE WAS A BOY — David Melton

GETTING STARTED

When I placed a sheet of paper in the typewriter and centered it, the white space seemed to overpower my words and thoughts. I stared at the keys of the typewriter. They were no help. "Leave us alone," they seemed to say. "Take your ideas somewhere else. Go out in the street and play."

I broke out in a cold sweat. I was stopped before I began. I started to suspect that becoming a writer might not be as easy as I had thought.

Then, I remembered that only a few blocks from our house, there lived a writer. He'd had more than twenty books published. I had read a couple of them and thought they were pretty good. I reached for the telephone book — not really thinking his name would be included because everyone knows famous authors have unlisted telephone numbers.

I made a note to myself: Get an unlisted number.

My eyes followed my paw down the list of Ms and to my surprise, I found his name — Melton, David — and next to his name was a number. So much for famous writers, I thought — but decided to call him anyway.

I dialed the number. I probably won't get past his secretary. Everyone knows famous authors never answer their own phones. They have private secretaries to handle their calls and make appointments.

I made another note to myself: Get a private secretary.

The phone rang several times and then a man's voice answered, "Hello."

"May I speak to Mr. Melton, please?" I asked

"This is he," the voice replied.

"Are you the David Melton who is the writer?"

"Yes," he said.

"My name is Ralph Miller," I told him, "and I am writing a book."

"How many pages have you written?" Mr. Melton inquired.

"Well, none yet," I admitted.

"Then, you aren't *writing* a book," he said. "You're just thinking about it."

"But I have the paper in the typewriter," I insisted.

"So, what can I do for you?" he asked.

"How do I start?" I suddenly blurted out.

There was a long pause and then he spoke again.

"Did you ever hear how Winston Churchill began painting?" he asked.

"No."

"Well, he started late in life," Mr. Melton told me. "Sir Winston had already been Secretary of the British Navy, had served terms in the House of Parliament and was known throughout the world. Anyway, he had always had an urge to paint and he decided not to put it off any longer. So, he had his secretary make a trip to the local art store and purchase the finest oil paints, the best brushes, an easel, a palette, and the largest canvas he could find."

"Does this have anything to do with writing?" I asked impatiently.

"It has everything to do with writing, Mr. Miller," replied Mr. Melton emphatically.

"Sorry," I said. "I'm sometimes all mouth."

"At any rate," Mr. Melton continued, Sir Winston set up his easel on the lawn of his country estate. He secured the canvas to the front. He remembered having learned in school that the three primary colors are red, yellow, and blue, so he opened the tubes of paint and squeezed out a portion of each on his palette. He looked at the large rectangle of white canvas that was set before him and he was suddenly struck with the feeling of stark terror."

"That's exactly what happened to me," I interrupted.

"Of course, it did," Mr. Melton said. "It happens to me every time I start a new book or a new chapter."

"What did Mr. Churchill do?" I asked.

"For more than an hour, he didn't do anything but sit and look at the canvas — which he later said had quite clearly and completely overwhelmed him."

"Then what happened?" I urged.

"Well," Mr. Melton continued. "That afternoon, Mrs. Churchill was having friends in for tea and, as one of the guests arrived, she happened to notice Sir

Winston on the lawn. Instead of going into the house, she walked across to where he was sitting. 'I say, Winnie,' she said. 'What do you think you are doing?' Sir Winston was quite annoyed and growled back, 'I'm painting. Can't you see?'

"The lady looked at the empty canvas and retorted, 'That's utter nonsense.' Without saying another word, she took the palette from his hand, swirled a brush through the globs of blue and red and yellow, mixing them all together into a brownish mess. Raising the brush to the canvas, she made several ugly marks across the surface. Then, she handed the palette back to the astonished Mr. Churchill and walked toward the house. Sir Winston said if he had not been so surprised he might have punched her in the nose or at least tripped her."

"But what did he do then?" I asked laughing.

"He looked up at the canvas and, when he saw the paint dripping down its surface, Sir Winston realized the woman had done him a great favor. She had done what he had been afraid to attempt. She had destroyed the power of the white. Sir Winston realized there was now no way he could make the canvas look worse. Anything he might do would only improve its appearance. He was no longer afraid, and he began to paint."

"But what does that have to do with writing?" I asked.

"Ralph, if I were in your room at this moment," Mr. Melton replied, "I would make large marks on your paper and destroy the power of the white. Since I am not there, you must have the courage to do it yourself. Of course, your marks will be letters and words. It makes little difference what those first words say. The important thing is that, as quickly as possible, you should type something — anything! You must destroy the power of the white."

"I will," I promised. "May I ask you one other question?"

"What is it?"

"Do you ever carry out the trash?" I inquired.

"Of course," Mr. Melton replied.

I thanked him for his help, hung up the phone, and made another note to myself: Writers are people too.

I did exactly as Mr. Melton had instructed. I immediately began destroying the power of the white paper. I started typing the first words that came into my mind — not worrying about sentences or paragraphs — but concentrating on thoughts and ideas.

I began to learn a lot about writing and books. I soon realized that a book is nothing but a patchwork of statements. A writer doesn't have to start at the beginning — he can write part of the middle, work on the ending, and come back to the beginning. The reader doesn't care which part was written first or second or even last. The writer is free to attack the work from any direction he chooses.

Why didn't someone tell me that writing is fun? Everyone had told me it was hard work. How little they know. Writing isn't dull or drab — it's the most exciting game in town. It's like playing mental ping-pong with the paper. You hit an idea to the paper and the paper smacks another idea right back at you. It's certainly more fun than playing Pac-Man because you aren't competing with some programmed game — you are competing with yourself, one on one. And if you don't like the rules, you can put another piece of paper into the typewriter and change them.

If everyone knew how much fun writing really is, television sets would be turned off by the millions and the sound of typewriters rat-a-tat-tatting would be heard throughout the land.

Soon, I became so engrossed in my work that I resented any interruption. When Mother told me dinner was ready, I was annoyed. When Dad stepped into the room and asked, "How's it going?" I wished he would leave me alone. If Jeff or Tim stepped in, I wanted to tell them to eat worms.

I wished I had gone to that mountaintop and found a typewriter. There, the only interruptions I would have had to endure would have been the muted sounds of crickets or distant thunder.

Reprinted by special permission from Independence Press.

THE CONFLICTING POWER
— Gary Jones, 17

The Best Ideas

I have one more piece of advice for beginning writers or those beginning any creative pursuit. I believe this advice is so important that I have it printed on a large card displayed prominently in my studio. At seminars and Workshops I place the card on a bulletin board and have students copy the words, urging them to place its message in full view. It reads:

THE BEST IDEAS
COME FROM THE WORK,
NOT FROM OUR HEADS.

All creative people know this to be true. Once you have destroyed the power of the white and you are writing and drawing or painting or whatever, a rather magic thing begins to happen which is rather spooky and wonderful. It seems as if great opportunities and ideas begin to form on the paper and the lines before you. New directions of plot or color burst forth and you begin to excitedly respond to the work. And you have no doubt that "God's in His Heaven and all's right with the world." You tend to drift into a state of creative euphoria. You are no longer laboring over the material; you have just been given a free ride. The creative brain has taken charge.

I have had English teachers tell me, "You'll be happy to know that I have my students write every day."

"For how long?" I want to know.

"For ten to fifteen minutes," they reply proudly.

Their efforts are commendable, but they have not made me happy at all. In fact, I am distressed to no end. I do all of my worst writing during the first ten to fifteen minutes. If we stop students at the end of ten or fifteen minutes, all we're doing is emphasizing that writing is difficult and worthless. We have got to give students enough time for the "magic" to happen if we are going to get them to joyfully and successfully write.

At this point, you should be no more than twenty minutes into the third session.

You have discussed the basic elements of a story.

You have suggested that "the best ideas come from the work, not from our heads."

Now instruct your students to write for the rest of the hour.

If you need to compose your master list of editors and art directors, you may do so while your students are writing. Then you may read the names aloud during the last five minutes of the session.

Once you have made the assignment to write, appear absolutely confident that your students are writing splendid stories.

Should any student say, "I can't get started," offer no sympathy. Just say matter of factly, "Of course you can — **Conquer the Power of the White.**"

Your Choice

If you are an elementary school teacher or one who has the same students during the following hour, then after a break, let them write and write and write. But do not count the second hour as one of the sessions.

If you are a teacher in a secondary school, at the close of the hour, assign them to finish the first rough draft of their text "tonight," and bring in the completed text to the next session.

Either way, the text should be written as quickly as possible, not allowing them enough time to write poorly. The pressure of a deadline is very important and urgency is their best ally.

Be sure to emphasize, at this point, spelling and punctuation are of little importance. Spelling and punctuation are functions of the academic brain. For now, we want their stories to come from the creative brain. The writers are not responsible for spelling and grammatical errors. These will be the responsibilities of the editors.

However, tell your students they should write with a dark pencil or a felt-tip or a ballpoint pen and keep the penmanship as legible as possible, because during the next session their editors will read their stories.

When my students use ruled pages, I insist they write on every other line to allow space for editor's and author's second thoughts.

No matter what kind of paper they use, they are to write on ONE SIDE ONLY.

In fact from this point on, whether they are writing or developing their illustrations, they are not to use both sides of any sheet of paper — **ONE SIDE ONLY.**

LETTER TO PARENTS

Now is a good time to inform parents of your project, welcoming any assistance they might contribute. As a professional writer, I'm apt to grab anyone who walks in the house while I'm working on a book, thrust stacks of pages into their hands and ask for their reactions. If they correct my spelling and punctuation or add super synonyms, I appreciate the help. However, if they make a suggestion with which I don't agree, I may choose not to use it, but I thank them just the same. Surely students should have the same privilege. Who cares where they learn to spell a word or punctuate a sentence, just so long as they learn?

Please note, this is only a suggestion letter. Alter it and rewrite it any way you choose. However, let me assure you if you invite the assistance of parents and tell them of this exciting project, they will truly appreciate your efforts and be most supportive for both the project and the students. Everyone will benefit, including the parents.

Dear Parents:

We have just begun an exciting project. Our classroom has been turned into a publishing office and, during the next _____weeks, each student will write and illustrate an original book.

As your author and illustrator of a forthcoming book is developing the manuscript and illustrations, please feel free to offer any suggestions and/ or alterations, or correct any spelling errors if he or she seeks your advice. As a professional person, he or she is free to elicit help or advice from whomever he or she should choose. It should also be understood he or she has the right to reject any suggestions made in regard to the creative work, including those made by me.

We hope you become as excited about this project as are we and look forward to a new edition for your bookshelf. As soon as plans are completed, you will be invited to attend an Author's Party to celebrate the unveiling of our students' books.

Best regards,
Your Name

SESSION 4

SUGGESTED LESSON PLAN

Teacher Preparation:

Reread all of Session 4.

Materials Needed:

Other than a copy of this book, none.

Activities:

Read aloud pages 46-50 to students.

Discuss qualities of good writing.

Time Required:

45 minutes

Assignment:

Complete rough draft of text.

GEE IF THE GUYS COULD SEE ME NOW
— Tim Herod, 17

Making the Pictures Clearer

Once your students are engaged in the writing process, they become eager receptors to bits and pieces of related information. They will now be more in tune to the plot and structure of stories and keen observers of the styles of writing. This is the perfect time for you to offer them additional information in regard to various formats of writing.

When offering students examples of writing formats, in order not to limit their creativity, we must be sure those examples are as widely varied as possible.

As we discussed earlier, it is imperative that you not reveal your personal preferences for a particular style or subject. As you read examples of students' writings to your class, if your students detect you favor one writing style over another or have special interest in a particular genre, some students will begin to alter their stories.

In recent years, one of the biggest deterrents to students' development of writing skills has been fewer opportunities to hear stories read aloud. In the days of radio dramas and when families read stories and books aloud for pastime, youngsters had wonderful access to experiencing story telling in very active ways. The spoken word suggested scenes and characters, but the listener, in his or her own mind, envisioned settings and action.

Famed monologist Joyce Crenfell says she has two nieces in England where radio dramas are still everyday occurrences. One niece is addicted to television, the other prefers to listen to the radio. One day the girl's mother asked her why she preferred the radio. Without hesitation the girl replied, ''Because the pictures are clearer.''

Since radio dramas are a rarity in our country and since fewer families read aloud in homes, I think more listening experiences should be provided in schools via recordings and teachers' reading aloud. Reading aloud is more commonly practiced in the elementary grades, but is almost non-existent in upper grades. Beyond grade school, students often are cheated of these vital learning and creative experiences.

You have an exceptional opportunity to offer them valuable information by reading the following excerpts to them:

Grabbing Readers' Attention

In his book, GEE, IF THE GUYS COULD SEE ME NOW, Tim Herod, seventeen years of age, begins his story with one of the most intriguing paragraphs I have ever read:

Hi. My name is Chuck. I like cars and grease, football and baseball, and Suzie Warner.

In her book, ALONE TOGETHER, Jenny Schroeder, seventeen years of age, immediately involves her readers with the action:

''Mamma, Papa, where are you?'' Ivy frantically screamed out the words, as she raced toward the fallen-down shanty which up until ten minutes ago had been her home. The tornado had destroyed the small Kansas farm on which Ivy's pioneer father, Bernard Halton, had struggled to support his family.

As she raced across the yard, Ivy tripped on a large branch which had been torn from their only tree, the cottonwood, and fell to the ground sobbing. Sable, her faithful dog, who had accompanied Ivy across the prairie to get the family's two precious cows, now nervously licked her hand, begging Ivy to get up and continue the search for her family.

And Jennifer Hill, age six, doesn't hesitate to introduce conflict in her book, THE EXCELLENT SWIMMERS:

Once there were two sisters named Katie and Vikki

who always wanted to swim.

But their mother kept saying, "No, no, no. Swimming is too much work and too hard work."

But Katie and Vikki (especially Vikki) kept saying, "Swimming is not too much work and we like to do hard things!"

But their mother kept saying, "No, you two are never going to learn to swim."

"Yes!"said Vikki and Katie.

"No!" said their mother.

"Yes!"

"No!"

"Yes!"

"No!"

It went on and on

Introduction of Characters

The best writers make their characters whole and complete.

In his book, THE LAST TORPEDO, eleven-year-old Doug Luther presents his characters in the midst of action and offers essential background:

It was a cold October morning when the boat set sail on its most important mission. It was to go from the northern coast of Germany to capture a British port. The boat had been well stocked for a long mission, and the crew was very eager to strike a blow for Germany.

As the boat left the harbor, Captain Muller, a tall, dignified man called a meeting of his staff. Captain Muller had been in the German Navy since 1930. He had more experience than anyone on board the ship. Captain Muller had attended the best military university in Germany. He was in his mid-40s. He had one child, a son, Henry. The last time the Captain had heard from Henry was three months ago. He was fighting with his platoon on the Russian front. The Captain was very proud of his son. They had talked about their military careers and the dangers that were a part of their lives. The Captain thought about these talks as he left.the harbor.

Navigator Franz Luther was a very experienced seaman. He had been guiding submarines throughout the war. He had never married. The sea was his life. He lived alone in a small apartment overlooking the wharf. From boyhood, he had looked forward to being in the Navy. His father had been a seaman in World War I and Franz had wanted to follow in his father's footsteps. He had become well known throughout Germany as an expert in his field. He knew the Atlantic Ocean like the back of his hand. He knew that he could guide his ship through any obstacle awaiting it. He was a quiet man and kept to himself most of the time. Later in this mission, the lives of the entire crew would depend on his knowledge of the sea.

When the boat started to turn east, a large dark shape loomed in front of them. It was the English battleship, *Victoria*. When the *Victoria's* leader, Admiral James Donn, saw the submarine, he ordered the battleship crew to commence firing on the boat.

Captain Muller called an emergency conference. They did not want to waste their ammunition on the battleship, but save it for their prime target. The navigator told the Captain that they could go under the water but would have to risk ice forming above them. This time of year ice would start to form and they would

be taking a big chance on surfacing quickly. They could only stay submerged for a week or two, because the boat's doctor warned that being under the ice for a long period would put a strain on the crew's mental and physical health. If any accidents occurred, they would need to surface and it would be impossible to get help.

The question was whether to submerge and risk being trapped under the winter ice in the North Sea or to be destroyed by the British battleship. At last, the decision had to be made . . . and it was made.

In UNCLE HERMAN — HERO UNAWARE, Henry Paustian, adult, builds the reader's interest in his central character before that character is even seen:

Uncle Herman was firmly established in my mind as a hero long before I met him. He was my father's younger brother and his name was mentioned often in our home. Some of my earliest recollections are vividly laced with my family's references to his unique experiences and personality.

There were several Uncle Herman stories that had become accepted by us children:

My father would say, "Uncle Herman was a hero in World War I."

He had won all kinds of medals but according to my father he shunned any reference to his bravery nor would he talk about the war.

Mother would say, "Uncle Herman has curly hair but he doesn't like it and he keeps running his fingers through the curls trying to straighten them."

My mother would laugh whenever she told us about Uncle Herman's reaction to his curly hair.

"Uncle Herman has a new *Reo Flying Cloud* and someday he will come and visit," my father would assure us.

Sure enough one summer morning he arrived. He came roaring up to our house in his big black *Reo* followed by a cloud of swirling dust. He stepped down from the running board, walked around to the passenger's side, opened the door and gallantly helped his wife — a petite, beautifully groomed, lady — out of the car.

Uncle Herman was wearing dark glasses and my mother didn't recognize him until he took them off. Then embarrassed, she laughed and remarked that she should have known him by his curly hair. Up went his hand to his hair and as predicted, he ran his fingers self-consciously through the curls.

I was only six years old, but I felt grown up as Uncle Herman shook hands with me and introduced himself and his wife, Aunt Dixie. She was the sweetest smelling, most beautiful lady I had ever seen. I was shy at first but they seemed so interested in me that I soon forgot my bashful feelings. I loved them immediately.

The time was the early thirties and we were at the height of two catastrophies that struck our farm community simultaneously — drought and depression. We didn't see people like Uncle Herman and Aunt Dixie; or clothes like they wore; or big fine automobiles like the *Reo*. We were used to battered *Model T Fords* and sun-scorched men and women with tired faces. The men wore faded, patched overalls and the women's house dresses were plain and worn.

Uncle Herman and Aunt Dixie took us riding in their marvelous automobile. As we drove through the nearby town, I sat between them feeling proud and important, waving to my friends as our powerful car roared past them. The *Reo* held a faint aroma of cigar smoke which, to me, added to its grand quality.

Uncle Herman and Aunt Dixie stayed for three wonderful days. On those summer evenings they sat and talked with my parents. As the night breeze began to cool the sweltering day, their voices blended with the chirp of crickets, the far away lowing of cattle and the call of whippoorwills. Lulled by these sounds, I drifted off to sleep.

Henry Paustian activates the reader's imagination through suggestion. Readers can actually visualize Uncle Herman and Aunt Dixie, picture what style and color of dress Aunt Dixie is wearing, and imagine what the *Reo Flying Cloud* automobile looks like. The writer gives no specific details of description. He only offers scant suggestions to our imaginations and we, as readers, fill in the details.

A Sense of Time and Place

In VIDEO MASTER, Tom Lynch, thirteen years of age, offers readers the opportunity to experience the character's feelings and adventures:

The boy stood at the front of the machine. His fingers rapidly worked buttons and one hand controlled a lever. His mind was set on only one thing — to beat the aliens.

He was so good at the game that he had been playing it for hours on just one quarter. And it was tiring. The bright lights and the loud blips of the machine were getting to him. He realized it was time to go home. Stepping back, he sadly watched his last starship explode brilliantly under the invaders' fire. He took a quick look at the new high score, then turned away.

That night as he crawled into his bed, he suddenly heard a voice in his head: "Ace, we need your help. You're our last hope. The video aliens are taking over the world. Be sure to go to the Arcade tomorrow. Our lives are in your hands."

Then everything went blank, and Ace fell asleep.

When he awoke the next morning, he thought about what he had heard. Surely it was a dream. But how could it be a dream if he was awake? He had to get down there fast!

He hopped onto his bike and sped off toward the Arcade. When he got there, he headed for his favorite machine, *Space Raiders*. As he put in a quarter, he felt a shocking feeling as a glow enveloped his body.

In AGE OF AQUARIUS, Brendan Shepherd, age twelve, offers a wonderful sense of time:

As the final minutes ticked off, a strange, eerie feeling came over me. What would happen if we got to Mars? Would we live? I tried to blot it all out of my mind.

Suddenly a voice came over the intercom, "T minus thirteen minutes to launch. Ignite first stage F 1 engines." More checks were made, some by voice, some by automatic instrumentation. I faintly heard the rush of propellants pouring into the huge tanks designed for thrust in the three stages. Metal crashed and pinged as the supercold liquids tortured it. We felt the movement

and vibration as thousands of tons of fuel and oxygen boiled and strained against the outer walls of the rocket.

"T minus 10 seconds and counting."

I said a hushed prayer under my breath.

"Seven . . .

"Six . . .

"Five . . .

"Four . . .

"Three . . .

"Two . . .

"One . . .

"Zero . . .

"Ignition!"

Thinking Process of Characters

Written material is the only media through which we are allowed to explore the thinking processes of characters.

Movies and plays are based primarily on physical action and spoken words of characters. In books and short stories, however, we have opportunities to journey into the minds of others.

In his book, AN EXERCISE IN SUSTAINED SUSPENSE, Chris Morrison, age fourteen, leads us into the thinking process of his narrator. In fact, Mr. Morrison has the courage to step where angels fear to tread by refusing to be intimidated by the unwritten rule in writing that all professionals know and by which they abide: Never write about writing because it makes for dull reading. But Mr. Morrison proves he has the skill to make both the writing and the thinking process as exciting as an inter-galactic battle:

He finished typing.

He leaned back in his chair, stretched and then popped his knuckles.

Then he yawned.

Tomorrow morning he would run for an office in the Student Council, and the speech that would get him there lay in front of him.

He read it carefully.

He reread it.

Then he read it again. He memorized as he went. He rehearsed it in his mind, accenting words here, slowing down on certain phrases there.

It would be very dramatic.

He imagined himself standing before a crowd of about six hundred kids.

A lone spotlight falls on him.

Silence pervades the gym.

He begins slowly. His words form in his throat and then neatly slide out of his mouth. At first, the audience will listen without interest. Then they will slowly begin taking notice, taking notice of exactly what words ARE slipping and sliding out so subtly.

Shock, disbelief. Then, he stopped his silly daydreaming. No, the boy corrected himself, nightdreaming. He read his speech one last time.

Satisfied, he folded the speech neatly in half and put it in his Social Studies folder so he would not forget it in the morning.

He had arranged to be the last speaker. That way

his speech would take them by surprise. It had to be that way because if he didn't take them by surprise they wouldn't feel the total effect of the whole thing. It simply would not work.

If he gave the speech somewhere in the middle or beginning it just wouldn't be the same. The audience of school voters would listen to the first six or so speeches — speeches that were woven with the threads of rayon unoriginality, polyester disinterest, and nylon boredom.

This was why he had to go last. The audience would be bored from listening to the first speeches. They would be off-guard, unwary. How appropriate.

His speech would hit them like a ton of bricks, take them by surprise, grab them by the neck and shake them until their teeth started to rattle.

Sneak attack.

No one knew him, either. All for the better.

"Who is this guy? He ain't got no right to say those things to us!"

Then who does have the right?

Then who will say those things?

The boy thought about this for a moment.

Things that should have been said a long time ago were finally going to be spoken in the school gym tomorrow.

And they won't be forgotten.

He made sure of it. He was going to tell them. All.

Setting the Mood

In PROMISES, Betty Lowrey, adult, creates the mood of her characters and lets readers feel the events of a warm summer day:

Mark sat under the old mulberry tree, hidden from his sister's view by the spreading branches of the snowball bush with its round clumps of white flowers. Momma had pushed him out the door as soon as he'd eaten, saying, "Go on now, mind yourself and be good. I've much to do." He could hear her putting away the breakfast dishes as he settled on the damp ground, digging with his chubby fingers down by the roots of the bush, examining the tiny black bugs and a couple of fat, white worms. It was his intention to stay out of Julie's sight, not wishing to help with her chores.

He maneuvered carefully around the rose bushes. Somehow roses and Momma went together. Just as he'd known, the radio clicked on bringing her favorite gospel program through the open, screened window.

"They that wait upon the Lord shall renew their strength," the minister's twangy voice cried out. "They shall mount up with wings like eagles. They shall run and not be weary. And they shall walk and not faint. Isaiah gives us many promises. Ours to receive."

"There you are!" Julie pounced upon her brother. "You come help me water Momma's petunias. You can carry a bucket as good as me."

"Darn it!" Mark mimicked his father, sliding to one side, pulling a rose thorn from his finger. "You made me stick that thing clear through my finger."

"You better shut up that cussin' — Daddy'll give you what for," Julie giggled, rolling her eyes.

The Richness of Detail

In THE SECRETS OF THE BERMUDA TRI-

ANGLE, Leo Garcia, eleven years of age, brilliantly moves the action ahead while filling in rich details of motivation of characters and the climate of a brooding storm:

Danny turned around and looked at his boss. "Do you really think I should take the airplane out today?" he questioned.

"It doesn't look that bad to me," his boss replied.

Danny looked at him, amazed, because his boss never missed the weather news in the morning. This morning the forecast was bad for flying.

"Heavy winds and rain in this area," Danny had heard them predict.

Danny sighed and got into the cockpit of his airplane. He pushed the ignition button. First the noise hurt his ears; then after a moment he got used to the roar of it. Soon he was up in the air, alone in a sky of heavy clouds. It seemed the clouds covered the earth with a thick gray blanket.

He was flying from Florida to Alabama to drop off some cattle that were already overdue by a full day. Perhaps that was why his boss had ignored the weather. It would take so much longer to drive them. "Oh well," thought Danny, "flying even in this weather would be better than listening to my boss nag about this or that all the way on a cattle drive."

The storm ahead became more violent and he could not fly around it. Suddenly he heard a loud sound. The rear rudder had been hit by lightning.

Believable Dialogue

In IT'S ALL HOGWASH, Susie Kemme, age fourteen, displays she has a true ear for believable dialogue, and has written some of the best conversation between teenagers I've ever read:

"I don't believe it," Kevin Taylor said. "Not again."

"It's true," Kevin's sister, Andrea, said. "Every weekend Mother does this. Why are you surprised?"

"I'm not really," he said. "Ever since she and Dad got divorced, she's been dating that gross guy who wears the toupee."

"You're not going to throw another party here tonight, are you?"

"Of course not, Andrea."

"Good. I'll have some company and some peace. Where are you off to?"

"Doug, Arnold and I are going out tonight."

"Why am I not surprised?" Andrea shrugged.

The phone rang and Kevin and Andrea raced to answer it. Kevin answered, looking pleased because he had gotten to the phone first, but it was for Andrea.

"Hi, Andrea." said Ginger Brown, one of Andrea's friends. "Just calling to see if your mother was going to be there this evening."

"Take a wild guess," Andrea said.

"Got a date?" Ginger asked.

"You're right. She left about an hour ago."

"I called to warn you that Patti is on her way over to your house. She told me that you needed to be bothered by someone, namely her."

"Oh no!" Andrea exclaimed. "Not the incredible Patti!"

As Andrea hung up the phone, she heard a knock at the door.

"What's the password?" she yelled through the door.

"Patti Ann Wilson is the cutest girl in the whole world!" Patti yelled.

"Hogwash! — But I'll let you in anyway," Andrea said.

"Oh, I like what you've done to the place," Patti said, looking around in the kitchen. "Kevin must have washed the dishes."

"With a knife in his back!" Andrea snapped.

Patti laughed. "Well, at least you got him to do them."

"Hello, Patti," said Kevin, coming down the stairs.

"Bye, Kevin," Patti quipped.

"Andrea, have you seen my new cassette tape?" Kevin asked.

"Nope," Andrea said. "Last time I saw it, it was in the living room."

"It's not there anymore," Kevin grumbled.

"Look in Mom's room," Andrea suggested.

"You're wearing too much makeup, Patti," Kevin said with a piercing look on his face. "You always wear too much makeup. It's weird."

"Speaking of weirdos, Kevin," Patti replied, "why don't you go look for your tape and leave Andrea and me alone."

Utilizing Style To Suggest the Historical Period

In THE SANDS OF PERIDUNE, Julia Thro, age nineteen, in style and technique of sentence structure, suggests the historical period of the narrative:

Those who have adventures are always called upon to tell their tales in taverns and in shops. So it is with me, but I have told of my encounter on the sands of Peridune so many times that I weary of the tale and of the memory. Therefore, I will tell the tale for the last time, and any who desire to know what really happened to the City of Ghosts may read it if they wish. It is a sad tale, but from it one may learn much.

To be sure, I never intended to go into the Peridune at all; I came there through another instance of the lack of prudence which marked my younger days. I was on the road in the month of Krali (that is May in the old tongue) with the intention of making some money in Sereli with my verses. A poet in those parts was rare, and I thought to enrich my coffers by drinking here, feasting there, and tossing off another verse for my dinner. What a life!

All went as planned my first four days there, although the keeper of the inn thought me a thief and eyed me constantly. That was grand — I, Remeric, a thief! A vagabond and a traveling poet, perhaps, but not a thief (not yet, anyway).

Proving young writers have the ability to understand and create the style of the period in a narrative, Colleen Brown, age nine, in her book, THE DWARF, offers the following:

A dwarf named Daker was sitting quietly in his home one night. When there was a knock at the door, he opened it. An old man named Ellsworth was standing there clad in white.

"Hail Daker, son of Dain," said the old man.

"What brings you here, wizard?" Daker asked.

"I have bad news from the south," answered the wizard.

"You must be kidding, Ellsworth," Daker remarked. "There has been no trouble in the south since the war."

"I know," Ellsworth agreed, "but now, there is a new problem. A fierce dragon has moved into the Elf Halls.

"Not the Elf Halls!" cried Daker. "Where did the elves go?"

"They fled to the forest," said Ellsworth. "You, Daker Toof, must come and lead a company of elves and dwarves to win back the Elf Halls and defeat the dragon. The dragon's name is Amundsen and he was sent by the Dragon Lord to kill the elves. Luckily they escaped before the dragon killed them."

Taking Chances

In one Workshop, a student, tongue-in-cheek, wrote as audacious a piece of humor as I have ever read. It was obvious to me he was taking a chance, but it was worth it.

As you will see, in his book, THE FIRST AND HOPEFULLY LAST BOOK OF SNAPJAWS, Robert (the Giff) Gifford, age fourteen, challenges the odds:

What is a snapjaw? For you uneducated dunces out there who don't know what a snapjaw is, I just might tell you. First sit down and shut up! Don't look at my book like that unless you want to be punched in the nose.

A snapjaw is a highly intelligent and quite peaceful creature. Although snapjaws are intelligent, they have an unbelievably moronic sense of humor and a very simple collection of body parts.

After reading the preceding examples aloud to your class, if you would like to add a couple of short selections of your own from published books, do so.

Instead of analyzing each selection of writing into boredom, through reading examples aloud, you have just given your students extremely valuable tools for improving their writing skills.

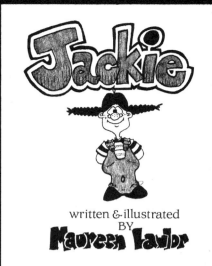

But Where Do All the Commas Go?

How To Edit Manuscripts

THIS AIN'T THE LIFE
— Kenny Church, 12

YOU CAN'T WIN THEM ALL
— Chad John, 11

As stated several times in this book, there is good reason for a writer not to be concerned with spelling, grammar and punctuation while completing the first rough draft of his or her manuscript. Since spelling is a function of the academic brain, but creative writing is a function of the creative brain, if we want our students to develop the most creative stories, we must allow their creative brains to prevail.

Even people who are normally good spellers find they jumble letters and leave out words, and even forget to cross their "t's" and dot their "i's," when writing a creative piece.

How many times have we been told to consult a dictionary if we don't know how to spell a word? If I went to a dictionary every time I couldn't spell a word while writing, I'd never finish the first page. And if students have to repeatedly open a dictionary, they will often stop trying to be adventurous with words, settling for those they can easily spell.

If we tell students that correct spelling is the responsibility of the editor, we remove such pressure and allow them to write freely and to explore language without the threat of their work being downgraded. Their writing will improve!

When Do Spelling, Grammar and Punctuation Become Important?

Spelling, grammar and punctuation become important before the final manuscript is prepared. When one of my manuscripts is sent to a publisher, I do everything in my power to make it letter-perfect. Not only have I reviewed and edited it, but it has been read by at least two other people. I do not want to cause the publishing editor to have to stumble over misspelled words or ragged sentences the first time he or she reads the manuscript.

SESSION 5

SUGGESTED LESSON PLAN

Teacher Preparation:

Reread all of Session 5.

Materials Needed:

Copies of Editorial Markings

Clean chalkboard and chalk

Activities:

Present proper editing approaches and procedures.

Present Professional Editorial Markings.

Offer examples of paragraphing.

Students edit manuscripts.

Time Required:

45 minutes

Assignment:

After manuscripts are edited, students are to review editors' comments and make necessary alterations.

THE HOUSE ON THE CORNER
— Angela Hunter, 11

Brian Clark, 13

The Editor's Function Is To Improve the Work

It is imperative that you guide your student editors toward making the most constructive changes and suggestions possible.

Write the following statement on the chalkboard:

> **The function of the editor is to improve the work;
> it is not to intimidate the writer
> nor to destroy the writer's confidence!**

Tell your students:

- If the editor finds a misspelled word, he or she should draw a line through that word, then spell the word correctly in the margin. Example:

  The dog ~~chazed~~ the cat.   *chased*

- If an editor thinks another word better suits the mood of the story, better defines the meaning or gives needed variety, he or she should circle that word, then write in a suggested synonym in the margin. Example:

  The colors of the rainbow were (pretty!) *beautiful*

- If the editor feels a sentence is not needed, he or she should cross **lightly** through that sentence.

- If an editor does not understand a sentence, he or she may ask the writer what is the intent of the sentence, or write in a suggested replacement in the margin.

- If an editor has suggested a number of corrections or changes in one section of the material, for ultimate clarity it may be wise for the editor to write out the edited section on a separate piece of paper.

- Of course, proper rules of spelling, grammar and punctuation must be observed at all times.

Now write on the chalkboard:

> **No editor has the right to write one negative word
> or comment on a writer's work.
> An editor should accentuate the positive!**

If the editor likes a certain sentence, he or she should give written comment in the margin of the paper. ***Terrific sentence,*** or ***Beautifully expressed,*** or ***Strong idea,*** or ***A bold concept,*** or ***Amusing,*** or ***Very touching,*** or ***Hilarious,*** or ***WOW!***

Stress to your students that it is unacceptable to ever write anything demeaning to the writer or his or her work, such as ***A stupid comment,*** or ***You're a terrible speller,*** or ***This story is silly,*** or any number of insensitive phrases editors might include. Instead, all comments and suggestions must be offered in the most positive and constructive ways.

Those writers who come up through the ranks of news reporting, magazine writing and advertising quickly learn their work is improved through judicious editing and abridging. In the printed media, space costs money and extra words and phrases are omitted with dispatch. A sentence or a paragraph which strays from the body of the work is cut. Once writers become less protective of their work and more receptive to constructive suggestions and deletions, their work rapidly improves. The *quality* of the finished product becomes the primary goal.

Encourage your students to carefully consider the constructive suggestions of their editors and make any changes they agree might improve the quality of the finished product. All of us have "thin skins" regarding our creative endeavors but when criticism is constructive and taken in the best spirit, our work cannot help but be improved.

David Vest, 14

Making Students Professional Editors

Editors in your publishing company should quickly learn professional editorial markings. You can either write them on the chalkboard and have them take notes or make copies of the following list for their use. THE MARKINGS ARE SIMPLE. The presentation and review should require only a few minutes. By the time the editors use each one a couple of times in editing their writers' stories, they will know them. Whatever you do — do not devise any kind of test for them. Remember, you are now working with professional people. If you treat these professionals as students, they may resign on the spot. There is nothing worse than being president of a company which loses all of its employees.

PROFESSIONAL EDITORIAL MARKINGS

CENTER:

Before: This line should be centered
in relation to the lines above and below it.

After: This line should be centered
in relation to the lines above and below it.

CLOSE-UP:

Before: The dog ran far away into the distance.

After: The dog ran far away into the distance.

COMMA:

Before: If you want a comma here mark it on the paper.

After: If you want a comma here, mark it on the paper.

DELETE:

Before: The girl sang a beautiful song.

After: The girl sang a beautiful song.

HYPHEN:

Before: She was a self reliant person.

After: She was a self-reliant person.

INDENT:

Before: The strong wind blew the boy's kite so high in the tree that he could not reach it.

After: The strong wind blew the boy's kite so high in the tree that he could not reach it.

INSERTS:

Insertions too lengthy to be written in neatly in the proper place, should be indicated by a "signal" line. This is usually done with a line to the proper place stating "Insert A" or "Insert 1" or any other *key letter* or *number* not matching those you have already used.

LET IT STAND:

Before: Many red and ~~golden~~ apples fell from the trees.

After: Many red and golden apples fell from the trees.

LOWER CASE:

Before: John caught sight of the RAINBOW.

After: John caught sight of the rainbow.

PARAGRAPH:

Before: A paragraph is indicated by a special mark so everyone will know where the changes are made.

After: A paragraph is indicated by a special mark so everyone will know where the changes are made.

PERIOD:

Before: The ring was set with diamonds and pearls.

After: The ring was set with diamonds and pearls.

QUOTATION MARKS:

Before: He said, No!"

After: He said, "No!"

SPACE:

Before: You can see whatis wrong here.

After: You can see what is wrong here.

TRANSPOSE:

Before: The kind best of candy is fudge.

After: The best kind of candy is fudge.

UPPERCASE:

Before: This word should be all capital letters.

After: This WORD should be all capital letters.

But Where Should We Paragraph?

Even those students who write well may have problems in knowing when to paragraph. I tell them two simple rules for paragraphing that seem to help:

Rule One: Each time a character speaks, paragraph.

"Little pig, little pig, let me come in," said the big bad wolf.

"Not by the hair of my chinny-chin-chin," replied the first little pig.

"Then I'll huff and I'll puff and I'll blow your house in!" the wolf howled.

Rule Two: Anytime you have more than six typewritten lines, paragraph. You'll be right more times than you'll be wrong.

Now this last suggestion may make the hair of English teachers stand straight on end and cause William Faulkner to turn over in his grave, but today we are used to reading *Time* magazine and newspapers. We have become accustomed to shorter paragraphs.

Put Your Editors To Work

Now have the writers give their pages to their editors. The editors should have the remainder of the hour to edit the writers' stories and to discuss their suggestions with the writers.

Remember —
No negatives!
Positive! Positive! Positive!
Terrific! Fantastic! Beautifully written!
Congratulations!

Pat Edwards

Dee Dee Strecker, 10

SESSION 6

Recopying the Work

While working with teachers who were testing these materials in a classroom setting, it became evident to us their students needed time to neatly recopy their stories to include all editorial changes required and/or preferred by the writers. This time also allows students to ask specific questions of their editors and gives teachers the opportunity to assist students on a one-to-one basis. You may even wish to utilize the assistance of more advanced students in helping those who are experiencing difficulties.

So, Session 6 is a very informal time for recopying materials, for teacher-student conferences and for editor-writer discussions. It is a session you should arrange to best benefit your particular class.

At the close of the session, you should inform your students to bring their art supplies to the next session because in Session 7 they will begin to develop their illustrations for their books. (Complete Supply List furnished on page 61.)

SUGGESTED LESSON PLAN

Teacher Preparation:

Make list of necessary supplies that students are to obtain.

Materials Needed:

None, unless you wish to give students a typed list of supplies.

Activities:

Students recopy stories.
Optional: Students receive individual help in recopying stories.

Time Required:

45 minutes

Assignment:

Gather needed art supplies and bring to next session.

ALBERT THE ARMADILLO·
— Sue Donaldson

SOMETIMES I WONDER
— Alisa Ferrell, 14

FRED, THE PING-PONG BALL NOBODY WANTED — Brildon Klingensmith

THE TEST— Jay Noyes, 15

ALONE TOGETHER — Jenny Schroeder, 17

HELL HOUSE — Carl Woolard, 17

WHEN THE CAN'TS CAN

If I've heard one person say, "I can't draw a straight line," I've heard thousands. What drawing a straight line and creative expression have in common, I've never known. Be that as it may, once these people start using a pencil or brush they are often astounded by their own abilities. What is even more amazing is that the styles and techniques of their illustrations are always so perfectly matched to the text of their books. All of the illustrations on this page were developed by people who claimed they couldn't.

A PUP WITH PERSONALITY
—Danny Harris, 11

SUPERMAC
— Rosemary F. Lumsden

THE ADVENTURES OF SIR LINDEN
— Michael Hood, 11

Neoma Boersma

Discovering the Book's Visual Personality

How To Lay Out Text Pages

THE BARONESS
— Jean Tucker

BE EASY, DADDY
— Ruthann Thompson, 17

The beginning steps of creating a book are much like meeting people for the first time — we see a face, we hear a voice and notice how the person moves and talks, but we don't really know that person. It isn't until we have been with new acquaintances for some length of time that we begin to enjoy the nuances of their personalities, are able to feel comfortable around them and, yes, even secure enough to openly express ourselves in their presence.

When I first begin a book, I hope beyond hope that somewhere in the first forty or fifty pages I will discover the personality of the work so that I can finally feel the nuances and shades of moods. Once the work takes on an individuality of its own, it can be dealt with as a reality, instead of just a string of words or pieces of color. Once that personality is secured, a greater understanding and excitement are infused into the editing, rewriting and development of the illustrations.

When your students finally discover their books' personalities, it will be fun, fun, fun for them and for you. No longer will their books be thought of or dealt with as a series of ideas but as total entities.

But I Can't Draw a Straight Line

The greatest thrill in teaching, I believe, comes at that instant when students discover they have extraordinary abilities they never even suspected they had. I feel privileged to witness these discoveries. People who never dreamed they could write suddenly find they can, and in short order are astounded at the caliber of material they can produce and how quickly their skills can be catapulted into the professional range. The same is true in drawing and painting — but what is really thrilling is that in visual arts the acceleration of their skills is often more dynamic and easier to see.

WHEN MIDNIGHT COMES
— Jonell Allen, 17
A

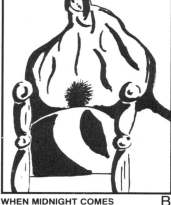

WHEN MIDNIGHT COMES
— Jonell Allen, 17
B

SIMEE
— Kay Hoffmeister
C

SIMEE
— Kay Hoffmeister
D

After the illustration assignment is made in the Workshops I conduct, at least six students will come to me in private and tell me they have taken the course because they want to become better writers, but they *are not artists* nor should I expect good illustrations from them.

In response, I always smile politely and tell them, "I understand. Don't worry about it." And they seem to relax, or at least semi-relax.

But there is always one who is more adamant about his or her artistic deficiencies. He or she stands before me with eyes filled with tears as if he or she is about to confess the darkest of secrets.

"I can't draw," he or she announces abruptly. "Is it alright if I make my story longer and not do any illustrations?"

"No," I answer. "All the books must be illustrated."

And then the bomb is dropped.

"Then I won't be back tomorrow," he or she announces.

"I'm sorry to hear that," I reply. "We'll miss you."

End of conversation.

Contrary to the tone of my reply, I do not take these conversations lightly. I spend a restless evening wondering if we will indeed lose that student. The following morning I endure anxious moments until I see him or her come through the doorway. And for some strange reason these doubters always return. I have yet to lose one — knock on wood!

The Symptoms Are the Same —
but What Do They Mean?

In my very first Workshop, one participant, Jonell Allen, said she would not return but came in the following morning with two illustrations which are of professional caliber. (Illustrations A and B)

Jonell said, "When I began work on these illustrations, I had the strangest sensation. It felt as if the top of my head opened up!"

"Do you mean you had a headache?" I asked.

"Oh, no," she explained. "It wasn't painful. In fact, it felt good — like pressure had been released, making me feel kind of light-headed."

"Hmmmm," I answered noncommittally.

In the second Workshop, Kay Hoffmeister, who needed the credits from my course to teach the following year, announced she could not draw and that she would not be back — credits or not.

However, the next morning she returned with magnificent drawings. (Illustrations C and D)

Kay told me she had experienced a strange sensation while working on the illustrations — "like my head opened up — a release of pressure. I felt light-headed, almost giddy."

When the course was completed, I asked Kay if she would duplicate her book for me so I could show it in other Workshops. Several weeks later, I received the original instead of the duplication. An enclosed note explained, "While I was working on my duplicate, my drawing improved so much that I decided to keep the second one for myself and send you the original. Hope you don't mind. After reading the note, I smiled, then chuckled, amused and joyful at my former pupil's success.

The experiences with Jonell and Kay made indelible marks in my mind. I knew I had observed something important, but I didn't know exactly what. When I saw the same thing happening with other students' work, I was delighted yet disturbed — delighted that their work would suddenly improve by leaps and bounds through several grade levels, but disturbed because I didn't understand the reasons why. Not until the following summer did I finally realize the answer.

During the Workshop in Lee's Summit, Missouri, Beth Blackwell, age 13, was working on illustrations for her book, TORN BETWEEN TWO FRIENDS. Beth was a methodical worker, very precise and definite in her approach. Although her book was sixteen pages in length, she had divided it into chapters and had designed very neat and attractive ornamentations around the chapter numbers with small, intricate illustrations. It was very capable work, but could hardly be called inspired or even daring.

Then one morning, Beth brought in three full-page illustrations she had done the previous evening at home. She asked if I would take a look at them because, as she put it, "they're not like my others."

When I saw them, I certainly agreed. They were not like the others. They had all been drawn and colored with the same felt tips and by the same hand, but these new illustrations were of a completely different style and technique. It was as if they had been done by another person or perhaps another personality.

Suddenly, for the first time I understood what I was seeing. The answer was so clear I wondered how I could have been so dumb for so long. On the table before me lay the results of the functions of two brains, each different from the other as day is to night. The neat and precise ornamentations had been drawn by Beth's academic brain. But the multi-images of brightly vibrant illustrations had been drawn and painted by her creative brain which had finally taken over. (Illustrations E, F and G)

I called to my daughter, Teresa, who was assisting me with the Workshops during the summer vacation from college, had her look at the illustrations and told her what we were witnessing. Teresa was as excited as I. We immediately began going from table to table, having the students lay out all of their illustrations. We could easily discern those which were academic brain illustrations and, in comparison, recognize those which were the product of the creative brain.

From that moment on, Teresa and I wore out shoe leather, walking from table to table, looking over shoulders, watching for the switches of the brains. The minute we would see a creative brain drawing or painting we would immediately tell the student how terrific it was and urge him or her to use the same technique on the other pages.

The books were improved by leaps and bounds. Soon students who were accustomed to drawing and painting on a fifth- or sixth-grade level would suddenly be working on a high school or even college level. Many students progressed the development of their work into the professional range.

As in writing, once we switch brains, the switch-over causes the creative brain to begin work automatically. We don't have to analyze composition or style because the creative brain intuitively understands style and composition. It has a thorough knowledge of space relationships and proportions and has an affinity for color and design. Once students switch brains, the Kay Hoffmeisters, the Jonell Allens and the Beth Blackwells, who may not think they can draw or paint, suddenly discover that not only **can** they do these things, they can do them extraordinarily well. Within our creative brains

A typical academic brain illustration.

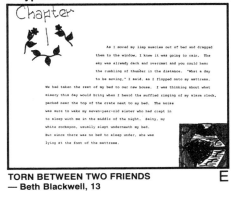

TORN BETWEEN TWO FRIENDS
— Beth Blackwell, 13   E

A creative brain illustration.

TORN BETWEEN TWO FRIENDS
— Beth Blackwell, 13   F

Another creative brain illustration.

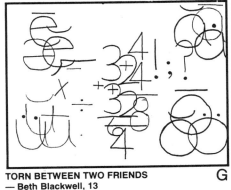

TORN BETWEEN TWO FRIENDS
— Beth Blackwell, 13   G

there are trillions and trillions of pieces of information. So vast is this reservoir of information that we cannot begin to imagine its scope. Not in just a few of us, but in all of us is the potential for creative genius.

POTENTIALS FOR GENIUS

If we were asked to name great artists, the first five who come to mind might in all probability be:

Leonardo da Vinci
Michelangelo
Rembrandt
van Gogh
and Pablo Picasso

I think there is little doubt that all five were creative geniuses, and few would argue the point.

But do you realize that due to the advent of movies, television and the availability of mass printed materials, most any child in the third grade has seen more visual images than da Vinci saw in his entire life? Every third grader has seen more uses of color and design, more decisions in composition, more types and styles of artwork and the results of more artists' work than da Vinci ever saw.

Every third-grade child has seen more creative images than Michelangelo saw in his entire lifetime. More than Rembrandt was ever privileged to see. More than van Gogh ever saw. And more than Picasso experienced.

Now if you would like to consider an even more astounding fact, consider that by the time children are in the third grade, they have seen more use of color and design, more decisions of composition, more types and styles of artwork, and the results of more artists' creative efforts than da Vinci, Michelangelo, Rembrandt, van Gogh and Picasso put together.

Surely, if any of these artists, whose knowledge and experience was certainly limited when compared to most third graders of today, could become creative geniuses, then we must begin to wonder, even dream, what our third graders and fourth graders and even twelfth graders might be able to achieve if they have the opportunity. That thought staggers the imagination with exciting possibilities.

Jenny Schroeder, 17

Wendy George

Vertical Books vs. Horizontal Books

You have probably noticed that a number of examples showing books written and illustrated by students in the Workshops are horizontal in format — wider than they are tall. However, all the information presented in this book tells teachers how to develop vertical books only. This is not an oversight on my part nor am I holding back information to write a sequel. In order to save teachers' sanity and to rescue students from making unnecessary mistakes, I have purposely not told you how to instruct your students to produce books in the horizontal format.

In my Workshops, I allow students the option of making a vertical or a horizontal book. I suppose, for the lack of a better reason, I like to live dangerously. To attempt both formats simultaneously means you have much more time and effort demanded of the teacher to provide two sizes of signature sheets and two sizes of paper for book jackets, plus individualized instructions to those students who choose to develop horizontal books. Worse still, students become confused. Some will look over at their neighbor's work which is on a different format, turn back to their own work and make their next illustration going the wrong way on the paper.

It you are willing to expend whatever extra time and effort is involved, don't mind surprises and can tolerate your students' frustration and confusion, then give your students the option of book development format, keeping the following in mind:

FOR HORIZONTAL BOOKS ONLY:

Signature paper must be trimmed, 22″ x 8½″.

Book jacket paper must be trimmed, 30½″ x 8½″.

Students must make layout sheets of their own, with the pages wider than they are tall.

PLUS, you must tell them they have to have a wide-carriage typewriter available to accommodate paper that is more than twelve inches wide.

Try it if you must. Do it if you can. I wish you the best of luck. You'll need it.

NECESSARY SUPPLIES FOR BOOK PRODUCTION

In the development of our students' books, up to this point they have not needed any special supplies. Before beginning Session 7, either you and/or your students should assemble necessary supplies for book production.

When I am conducting a WRITTEN & ILLUSTRATED BY...WORKSHOP, I supply signature paper for gluing and final assembly of the students' books, and also the 8½-inch by 11-inch pieces of cardboard which are used as templates to lay out pages and eventually become stiff covers for the books. All other supplies, such as pens, pencils, colored felt tips, water colors, glue sticks and sketchpads are obtained by the students. (Some of these supplies many students already have.)

Because schools have different procedures for ordering and alloting supplies, and have certain stipulations regarding what materials students may be asked to furnish, in order to complete a WRITTEN & ILLUSTRATED BY...WORKSHOP, a teacher may have to make some essential adjustments in acquiring supplies. Many times the PTO, service organizations and even businessmen and women in the community are helpful in sponsoring and funding special projects like the Workshops.

Be that as it may, in gathering the needed supplies for the development of books, I will list the materials and items required for the Workshops and also suggest alternative materials.

SIGNATURE PAPER

70-pound or 80-pound white offset can be obtained from a local printer, trimmed to size. It is a relatively inexpensive paper. If you tell your printer it is needed for a class project, he or she may even donate the required number of sheets.

Size: 17″ x 11″

Number of Sheets Per Student: Six (6), but get several extras for mistakes.

Alternative: Manilla drawing paper, trimmed to size.

BOOK JACKET PAPER

Obtain 70-pound to 80-pound white offset from your local printer who will probably be willing to donate this supply.

Size: 25½″ x 11″

Number of Sheets Per Student: One (1), but get extras.

Alternative: Manilla paper, trimmed to size.
(If the 25½″ width is a problem, two sheets may be glued together at the spine of the cover during the last stages of assembly by the students.)

Note: Signature sheets and jacket paper should not be passed out to students until these are needed.

CARDBOARD (Chipboard) FOR COVERS

(Which will also be used as templates for outlining pages of books)

Again, your local printer will probably have sheets of chipboard on hand and will trim them to size.

Size: 8½″ x 11″

Number Per Student: Two (2), but get extras.

Alternative: Stiff posterboard that can be trimmed to size.

Note: One piece of cardboard should be passed out to each student to use as a template; the other piece should be given to students later when they are ready to glue on the covers of their books.

SKETCHPAD

9″ x 12″; One (1) per student. *Suggested Brands:* Mead, Middlesex, or bp Raritan.

Alternative: Manilla paper, trimmed to 9″ x 12″ or larger.

GLUE STICKS

Three (3) per student. *Suggested brands:* Dennison, Pritt, or UHU Stic.

Alternative: Standard white paste, which must be *carefully* spread on the paper so lumps are not left and then allowed *necessary time* for drying.

COLORED FELT TIPS

Come in sets, both wide-tip and thin-tip. *Suggested brands:* Crayola, Marvy, and Carter's.

Note: I strongly recommend that your students use felt tips for their illustrations because the finished products are often superior in appearance and the boldness of the strokes is sure to elicit creative brain activity.

DRAWING PENCILS   HB and 2B

Note: If some of your students want to develop pencil illustrations for their books, they should not attempt to use ordinary writing pencils, but must obtain both HB and 2B drawing pencils so the drawings will be dark enough to be easily seen. Those students who use pencil must also get a can of spray fixative (for pencil) and spray their their illustrations BEFORE their pages are pasted onto the signature pages.

BINDERY SUPPLIES

Large Needles, Carpet Thread, and Push Pins. One (1) per student (may share).

MISCELLANEOUS

And of course, students should have other basic supplies such as Scissors, Pencils, Rulers, Erasers, and Typing Paper.

NOTE:

The teachers who tested the manuscript of WRITTEN & ILLUSTRATED BY... found it advantageous to have each student obtain an expandable folder in which he or she could store and carry their book supplies and materials. Or by folding large sheets of paper and gluing the sides, your class could construct their own briefcases.

LAYOUT SHEETS FOR TEXT PAGES

Title _____ Illustrator _____

BEGIN TEXT

0   COPYRIGHT   1

2   3

4   5

6   7

8   9

10   11

12   13

14   15

Pages 0 through 15

For now, you and your students only need to be concerned about the pages that are numbered from 0 through 15. These pages are reserved for the text and the illustrations.

We will deal with the Title page and other opening pages later. Until students have developed the materials for text pages, they should not even think about Title pages, etc. They must first become familiar with the personality of their books before designing front matter or covers.

Although we are aware that "0" is not a number, for the sake of the books, let's pretend that it is. Therefore, "0" through "15" really comprises sixteen pages.

If we are going to be consistent with professional publishing practices, the first page of text is always printed on a right-hand page and is numbered page "1." Therefore, all right-hand pages in printed books have odd numbers — 1,3,5,7,9, and so on, and all left-hand pages are even-numbered — 2,4,6,8,10, etc. If you wonder why printers number pages like this, I'll tell you — I don't know. And I don't think we'll ever find the real reason. Having asked a number of printers and publishers why pages are numbered in this fashion, I've been given a number of reasons, all of which boil down to the fact: *pages are numbered this way because they are numbered this way.* Perhaps in years past, Gutenberg or someone set this precedent and through the years it has become traditional.

When I am writing and illustrating a book, I draw out in miniature the number of pages the book will contain. Then, as fast as I can, I scribble free-hand lines to indicate typed matter and squiggly circles for illustrations, as shown in the right column.

In a matter of minutes, I have a good idea of the space relationship of the elements in the body of the book.

There is no magic trick to the process except the faster it is performed, the better. If we slowly lay out the pages, we will allow the academic brain to lay out the book. Although this preliminary work will be neat and orderly, it will also tend to become dull, dull, dull! Remember, the creative brain loves quick and spontaneous activities and one of its prime functions is to visualize holistic approaches.

You See — It's Easy!

When the class has assembled, tell them they are about to lay out the text of their books.

Distribute the Layout Sheets and tell your students to write in the titles of their books and their names in the spaces allowed at the top of the sheet.

Explain that, for now, they should not be concerned with the pages that are labeled with letters. Today, they will lay out only those pages labeled from 0 through 15. The lettered pages will be laid out at a later time.

Then go to the chalkboard and show them how to lay out the pages of text and illustrations. Begin drawing, as you say:

"I'm going to place my first typed text on page 1 — line, line, line.

SUGGESTED LESSON PLAN

Teacher Preparation:

Make copies of Layout Sheets.
Draw pages as shown on Layout Sheet on the chalkboard (do not have to be measured precisely).

Materials Needed:

Copies of Layout Sheets, one per student but should make a few extra.
Cardboard templates (which will also make one cover).

Drawing paper, if you are furnishing it, and any other supplies you have decided to furnish.

Activities:

Demonstrate method of drawing layouts in miniature.
Have students lay out pages 0-15, as directed.

Time required:

45 minutes

Assignment:

Students develop and complete two illustrations for their books.

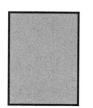

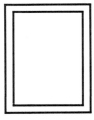

"First illustration on facing page 0 — the one with the copyright information at the bottom — squiggly, squiggly, squiggly.

"An illustration on page 2 —

"Type on page 3 —

"A half-page illustration on page 4, with type below —

"A full-page illustration on page 5 —"

And so forth, as the mood strikes you.

Draw as fast as you can talk. In less than a minute, you have laid out the placement for type and illustrations on the pages.

When you finish, tell the students they are to lay out pages 0 through 15 using either pencil or ink pens — NOT WITH LIGHT MARKS, BUT WITH DARK, BOLD STROKES. Dark, bold strokes will call forth the creative brain, while little light pencil marks will come from the academic.

To insure you have the creative brain's attention, tell the students:

"You have **three minutes** to lay out pages 0 through 15 — START!"

You time them.

Add some pressure by saying:

"You now have **two minutes.**"

Add more pressure:

"You now have **one minute.**"

"Time's up. **Stop.**"

"Congratulations. You have now laid out the text of your book."

The Drawing Begins

As soon as the layouts are completed, give every student one of the 8½" x 11" cardboards. Show them how to use the cardboards as templates.

Place the template in the center of a page (there should be an excess of paper showing on all four sides). Holding the template steady and in place, each should draw a line with a pencil all the way around the template, which will give an outline of the page size of the finished book.

Tell the students they should use the template to draw an outline on every page in their sketchpads (or on their sheets of drawing paper) before they begin any illustrations. Now allow them time to do this outlining which should require no more than ten minutes.

After they have finished outlining all the pages, be sure to tell them they should use ONLY ONE SIDE. They should never do any work on both sides of any sheet of paper. EVERY ILLUSTRATION SHOULD BE ON ONE SIDE ONLY.

Now tell them to begin to develop their first illustration. It does not have to be the first illustration indicated on page 0 of their layouts. They may choose any illustration — first, middle or last.

Be sure to remind them, since they are developing a vertical book, that each page will be taller than it is wide.

Now back off and let them work.

Before the session closes, tell them they are to complete two illustrations by the next session.

If you have the same group of students the following hour, be sure to give them time to get up and move about for at least ten minutes. Then, if you like, allow them to work on their illustrations during the next hour. This hour will not be counted as one of the sessions.

Otherwise, the development and completion of the two illustrations will be considered homework.

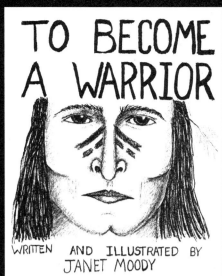

TO BECOME
A WARRIOR

WRITTEN AND ILLUSTRATED BY
JANET MOODY

7
Turning Illustrations into Visual Wonders

The Function of Art Directors

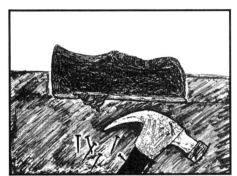

THE ADVENTURES OF OLIVER
— Aaron K. Benson, 11

ALPHA CENTAURI IV
— Steven Fausett, 15

I used to believe only a select number of artists had an aptitude for illustrating books. But since observing children develop their own books, I am convinced that regardless of what level of drawing skill each possesses, all children have a terrific, innate sense of the elements of a good book illustration. More precisely, once students switch to their creative brains, the composition of their artwork becomes spontaneous and right.

Criterion for a Good Book Illustration

A good book illustration urges the reader to read the story.

It is as simple as that, and you will not have to discuss styles of art nor intent of subject with your students. As with composing titles for books, students intuitively understand what's right. It's amazing! And any additional discussion or analysis we might force upon them will, if anything, involve needless time and only confuse the issue.

The only point we really need to stress to students, especially those who are timid about drawing or those who lack self-confidence, is to advise them to throw caution to the wind and commence drawing more boldly and making their lines stronger. Everything else will fall into place.

To get students to work boldly, insist they draw with their HB or 2B soft lead pencils or felt tips. It is the academic brain that will draw lightly. By insisting your students draw with bold lines, most will quickly shift to their creative brains. The creative brain knows no fear nor inhibition. It will bear down on that lead.

And Draw It Faster!

Important! Important! Important! Anyone who is having trouble drawing should be told to draw **faster**. The faster one draws, the better the drawings will be. Slowness only allows the academic brain to interfere.

When students draw slowly, the academic brain tries to measure everything, making the figures appear stilted, but when students draw quickly,

LAST WARRIOR
— Robert Duckett, 15

the creative brain places everything into perspective and order of importance.

If one student has trouble drawing, let's say a wagon, tell him or her to draw it quickly, in no more than fifteen seconds. Both you and your students will be surprised at how well the wagon will be drawn.

Remember, the creative brain has stored trillions and trillions of pieces of visual information. When it is allowed to take over the drawing, it will immediately supply the necessary images for the artist. You will see. It really works.

Although you may not consider yourself an artist, you probably know twice as much about drawing and painting as you think you do and you know a million times more about drawing and painting than you might suspect.

If these statements don't ease your mind, let me tell you a secret. If you only tell the students to illustrate their books, show them the layout forms, tell them what kinds of paper to use, and leave them absolutely alone and on their own, they, in turn, will design and illustrate beautiful books. It is truly a no-fail system.

Some of you may consider having an art teacher take over the design and illustration sections of the book development. I urge you not to do so. While some art teachers have a thorough concept of book design and format, others simply do not and will only confuse your students. As you will see, I will provide you with easy-to-follow instructions. If you pass the information on to the students, they will come through with flying colors — I promise!

SESSION 8

SUGGESTED LESSON PLAN

Teacher Preparation:

Reread all of Session 8.

Materials Needed:

Only the art supplies you furnish.

Activities:

Discuss function of art directors.

Show and discuss ways to improve students' illustrations.

Discuss format for typing stories.

Time Required:

45 minutes

Assignment:

Complete three illustrations.

Have stories typed.

By Session 8 your students should have completed at least two illustrations.

Now is the appropriate time to instruct art directors of their duties.

Write on the chalkboard:

> **The function of an art director**
> **is to improve the work of the illustrator;**
> **it is not to intimidate nor destroy**
> **the confidence of the illustrator.**

No negatives!
All positives!

When art directors view illustrators' work, they should look for three things:

1. Will the illustration encourage the reader to read the text?
2. Can the drawing or painting be seen from a distance of six feet? (This is an important consideration because it encourages students to draw boldly.)
3. How can the illustration be improved?

It is now time for an art director-illustrator conference to allow the art director to review the illustrator's work and make any suggestions for improvement.

"Wow! That's terrific!" is always a good starter for the art director-illustrator conference.

If the art director decides the illustration is acceptable, he or she should sign his or her name in the bottom margin.

If an art director makes suggestions for improvements, he or she should tell the illustrator. The illustrator may use the suggestions or not.

After art director-illustrator conferences, it is time for *show-and-tell.*

Have students lay their illustrations on their desks so you can quickly walk past and see them. Beginning with some of the best illustrations, hold these up for the class to view. Remind your students, in a good illustration all the main elements should be visable from at least six feet away.

Once you make that point, ask the class how the artist can improve the work.

Their suggestions will primarily consist of:

''Make the figures bigger.''

''Make the lines stronger.''

In a matter of seconds, everyone will get the idea and their comments will serve to reinforce the suggestions of the art directors. As you continue to hold up illustrations, even the artists will start saying, ''I should make the faces bigger'' or ''the lines stronger.''

By holding up the students' work, you have demonstrated to all members of the group that their work is going to be seen. Students who otherwise might become complacent in their work, will now attempt to improve their style and technique without you having to badger them. Acceptance and praise from other students, and ultimately from readers, will be uppermost in their reasoning.

After the students have reviewed and commented on each other's work, you may wish to show them one of the simplest ways artists can improve their illustrations.

BRAIN STORM
— Kim Volskay, 17

INDIANS ATTACK DEADWOOD
— Clint Kajinami, 12

A Quick and Easy Trick for Improving Illustrations

When all the lines in a drawing are of the same thickness, they are boring and flat. Any drawing can be improved, not by one hundred percent, but by a thousand percent, in only three or four minutes by adding **emphasis strokes.**

When the artist emphasizes each corner and curve of the figure with a bolder stroke, the figure stands out better. What is even more significant, as the lines vary in boldness, the figure seems to breathe. What is really happening is, without realizing it, the viewer's eyes are trying to connect the lines, which adds a sense of action to the figure.

The same holds true for inanimate objects.

Now allow the illustrators to work on their illustrations.

While students are working on their illustrations, you have the opportunity to review their edited manuscripts and make additional suggestions — all of which must be done in a very positive manner.

By the time your students have completed two or three illustrations, you should begin seeing some extraordinary works, even from those who previously felt such talents were nonexistent for them. It isn't at all unusual for these students to discover their talents and become so excited you can barely contain them in the classroom. Often they become extremely hy-

THE UNDERGROUND CITY
— John Townley, 12

THE PROTECTION OF BILLY BOB
— Randy Summervill

"The lattice drew you here. It has become part of you. It is my job to join you with Asstroth, as my companions are," he said, gesturing to the things standing behind Dan.

"But, I enjoy chess, I will make a proposition. We will play a game of chess. "f I win, your 'death' is sealed. If you win, I will go in your stead." Obviously he had no fear of his master.

The lattice things led him over to a table upon which sat a beautiful black-and-white marble chess set, but the figures were wrong, different. They were fantastic, at best - demonic, at worst, representations. Necrom took the white pieces, leaving Dan with the black.

The white pieces facing him were frightening. All of their eyes seemed directed at him. The illusion chilled and unnerved him. Dan believed he caught one making a rude remark to him.

"You have the first move," said Necrom diplomatically.

The game was fevered, for the pieces seemed possessed of a will of their own. Positions changed by themselves, but Dan was winning. He was a survivor. HE WAS A SURVIVOR!

"A break?" asked Necrom after several hours of play. Dan was winning, but that lead was measured by pieces per hour.

"Certainly," replied Dan.

The pieces stopped their movement and both players leaned back in their chairs.

"I'm going to win," said Dan, matter-of-factly.

SURVIVING LATTICE
— Brian Clark, 13

All typing should be double-spaced. Typists should allow 1″ margins at top, bottom and both sides of every sheet.

peractive, even aggressive, in their work and begin to make daring experiments with techniques and styles. Their enthusiasm is infectious. Students begin to react to each other's work with a great deal of interest and generosity. The atmosphere of the room becomes a strange mixture of friendly competition and unabashed encouragement.

While the academic brain is a gold mine, an oil well and a diamond field combined, the creative brain is jam-packed with atomic energies, ready to explode with exciting ideas once the opportunities are presented. The slogan printed on matchbook covers proclaiming "Anyone can draw," may very well be true. For surely, if there is anyone who cannot draw or paint, I have yet to meet that person.

Have the Stories Typed

Once the stories have been edited and you have reviewed them, it is time to have them typed. I realize getting students' work typed may pose some problems in finding typists.

Even though some students in secondary school will be able to type their own stories, **they should not.** All stories should be typed by someone other than the writers. This is extemely important.

Some teachers line up parent volunteers to do the typing; others leave it up to the students to get their own secretaries. But if you want your students' work to improve, students must sense their writing is important enough to be typed. When someone else does their typing, you will find that the writers begin to do the very thing you want. They will become extremely sensitive to spelling and punctuation and will be eager to improve their stories. They will become professionals in the proper sense. And a hugh burden is taken off your back.

I have students come up to me and say, "My typist misspelled a word on page 3. Do you think it should be retyped?"

"That's up to you."

"Do you think anyone will notice?"

"What do you think? It's your book. How perfect do you want your finished book to be?"

I have little doubt most writers will determine all errors be corrected and retyped. If the student doesn't have to do the retyping, he or she will not have to expend energy or time on corrections. The students can apply their efforts to illustrations and formulation of the final products.

I had one irate student storm into the Workshop one morning and slam down his papers in disgust on the desk.

"What's the matter with you?" I asked.

"I just fired my mother," he replied, holding out his papers. "Look at these mistakes! I'll have to get someone else to type my book."

And he did.

The first typing should be double-spaced, with at least a one-inch margin on each side and at the top and at the bottom of each page. The text should be typed in a continuous flow. The student will later be given the opportunity to decide how the sections will be divided and paged in his or her book.

At the end of Session 8, assign students to complete three more illustrations before the next session.

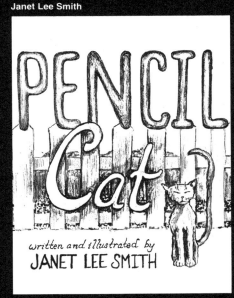

8

The Glorious Adventures in Packaging the Product
How To Design Book Jackets

SUGGESTED LESSON PLAN

Teacher Preparation:

Reread all of Session 9.

Select ten books as examples of jacket design.

Materials Needed:

Cover paper

Glue

Scissors

Cardboards (for templates)

Activities:

Show students how to lay out book jackets.

Show good jacket Front designs and discuss.

Students design Fronts of jackets.

Time Required:

45 minutes

Assignment:

Make necessary improvements to Fronts of jackets.

Complete all illustrations on text pages 0 through 15.

After the students have written and edited their stories and have completed at least five of their illustrations, they now know the personality of their books and are ready to consider the front area of their book jackets.

The front of a book jacket might be viewed as a poster or an advertisement for the book. Although we are told time and again not to judge a book by its cover, we realize the cover of a book is what first stimulates our imaginations and influences our selection of a book for reading.

There are five areas of a book jacket:

BACK FLAP	BACK	SPINE	FRONT	FRONT FLAP

For now, let's concern ourselves with only the Front.

Although the hard covers of most printed books are slightly larger than their pages, in our handmade versions, covers and pages will be the same size in order to act as guides for marking the dimensions of the pages. So, students will use their cardboards as templates for laying out the dimensions for both the Front and the Back of the book jacket.

Ivor Burgesser

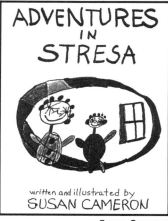

— Susan Cameron

The Front

Fronts of book jackets should contain four elements of information:

1. **Title of book;**
2. **An illustration;**
3. **The line or lines, "Written and Illustrated by";**
4. **The name of the author/illustrator.**

You should select at least ten books from the library that have book jackets. As examples of well-designed Fronts, show them to your students and discuss the ways the designers have arranged the elements of information effectively. (You might even like to throw in a couple of poorly designed jackets for comparison.)

The criteria for well-designed jacket Fronts are:

- **The title is easy to read;**
- **It is bold enough to be read at a distance of six feet;**
- **The design and style should suggest the subject and mood of the book;**
- **All the elements should look at home in the space without crowding one another or competing with each other.**

Take five to ten minutes and discuss the jacket Fronts of the sample books. Have your students point out the advantages of each one and the disadvantages — those which are difficult to read or do not fit the mood of the text.

Now instruct them to design the Front of their book jackets on a page in their sketchpads (or on drawing paper) which has already been outlined for size, just like those pages used for illustrations.

Tell them they have **twenty minutes** to complete their jacket Fronts. "Begin."

After fifteen minutes have elapsed, tell them they have **five minutes** to finish.

Then stop them when the twenty minutes are up.

Now take the next five minutes to hold up each jacket Front and offer the artist suggestions for improving the Front.

"Make the lettering easier to read."

"Make the illustration bolder."

"Make the name of the writer and illustrator larger," (or "smaller," as the case may be).

"Keep the work away from the edge of the paper."

Before the next session, students should make necessary improvements on their jacket Fronts and finish all illustrations for pages 0 through 15.

Final Typing

Since the students have now completed all their illustrations on pages 0 through 15 and are presently working on their book jackets, now is the perfect time for them to have their completely edited stories typed. Since these are final pages that will appear in their books, they **should not be typed on regular typing paper** because it is often too thin and too absorbent and may wrinkle when the glue is later applied. Students should take enough outlined pages from their sketchpads (or use drawing paper) and instruct typists to type the finished pages **only on the sketchpad paper or the drawing paper.**

IF some of the students have decided to include illustrations and text on the same pages, advise them to mark the area where the typing is to be placed **before** they put their final illustrations on these pages, just in case the typist should make mistakes or inadvertently ruin a page. After the typing is correctly completed, the student can then draw or paint in the illustration. If the student should ruin a page or is not satisfied with the results, he or she should be allowed to have the page retyped and begin again.

Copyright

The Copyright page is very simple. It requires only one line be typed in at the bottom of the page, at least 1/4-inch from the cutoff. The line should state the appropriate year and the student's name:

Copyright 1985 by <u>Student's Name</u>

Instruct students to have the Copyright line typed on the bottom of their first illustration which is on page 0.

How To Complete the Book Jackets

As soon as Session 10 begins, again review the book jacket Fronts and ask for suggestions for improvements.

Once the suggestions have been made, stress that the jacket Front is one of the most important elements of a successful book.

However, tell your students they have the right to decide whether or not they wish to take the suggestions and make the necessary improvements. The decision is strictly in their hands (which they will be greatly surprised to hear). Once you offer them this decision-making freedom, **DON'T, DON'T, DON'T** be tempted to interfere or make wild or veiled insinuations of lowered grades, or resort to needless sarcastic remarks. WRITTEN & ILLUSTRATED BY...WORKSHOPS are as much a course in decision making as they are in book design and development. Do not cheat your students of the experience of having to make as many of their own decisions as possible.

The Back

The Back of a book jacket can be designed in a variety of ways. It may contain:

1. **A picture of the author/illustrator** — the more glamorous or studious, the better; or
2. **An illustration** — either full-page or smaller; or
3. **Reviews of the book.**

The third alternative is an interesting one. When twelve-year-old Karen Kerber had completed her book, WALKING IS WILD, WEIRD AND WACKY, she asked, "What are the nice things that are sometimes written about books that are placed on the backs of books?"

"Oh, you mean reviews?" I asked.

SUGGESTED LESSON PLAN

Teacher Preparation:

Reread all of Session 10.

Materials Needed:

Only the art supplies you furnish.

Activities:

Instruct students to edit their typed pages and explain how to have the text typed on their sketchpad or drawing paper.

Discuss the elements of book jackets.

Have students begin designing and writing the elements of their jackets.

Time Required:

45 minutes

Assignment:

Complete all elements of their book jackets.

BENJAMIN GOES AWAY
— Kathy Ryan, 11

JO JO FINDS A FRIEND
— Lisa Bohanon, 12

FRONT FLAP COPY

ASHES IN THE WIND is a stirring, beautiful collection of poetry about teenage feelings, by a teenager.

In this, his first book, Philipps uses vivid, captivating illustrations, combined with shockingly on-the-mark poems to create a collection that both teenagers and adults will enjoy and be affected by emotionally as the true meaning of the poems comes across. The book provides a rare look at the way teens view their world—a view not often found in print.

The style of ASHES IN THE WIND is on a level with many top-notch, well-known poetry collections in print today, such as LEAVES OF GRASS and PEPPER AND SALT. Certainly, it would make a marvelous addition to the library of any sensitive lover of poetry.

**from ASHES IN THE WIND
— Tim Philipps**

BACK FLAP COPY

ABOUT THE AUTHOR

Seventeen-year-old Jenny Schroeder is an animal lover. She has been a 4-H Club member for ten years. She has had a pet parakeet, dog, horse and several sheep as some of her projects. She has also been interested in birds and other nature projects. Volley ball ranks high on her list of priorities. She will be playing on the Goessel High School volley ball team for the fourth year. As a senior she will be co-editor of the annual. She enjoys writing and entered an agricultural news reporting contest in FFA, an organization of which she has been a member throughout high school. She placed fourth in the state of Kansas in this contest. She lives in a rural Goessel country home with her parents, Jerry and Darlene Schroeder, and her dog, Lucy, her cats, Benjamin and Gizmo, her horse Dusty, and her nine sheep.

**from ALONE TOGETHER
— Jenny Schroeder**

"Yes, she agreed. "How do the publishers get those?"

"Well, they usually send copies of the book to newspapers and magazines where book reviewers read them, then write comments as to their opinions of the book."

"If I took my book down to *The St. Louis Post-Dispatch* office, do you think they would review it by tomorrow morning?" she wanted to know.

"I don't think that would be enough time."

"Then how would I get the comments?"

"Write your own," I suggested.

She did. You might notice that by the time she finished writing her own reviews. *The St. Louis Post-Dispatch* was reduced to fifth place.

An excellent book for the stimulation of the mind.
— New York Times

A superior book for all ages...
— Newsweek Magazine

This book is foot-stompin' good!
— Atlantic Monthly

A classic book for entertaining people of all ages.
— Book of the Month Club Selection

So excellent it will set your mind jogging.
— St. Louis Post-Dispatch

I would like to point out that Karen's efforts not only gave her the opportunity to study review format, but also to investigate those sources considered the most influential in reviewing books. That is meaningful research.

Students should be given free choice of which format to use for the Backs of their jackets.

The Front Flap

In the marketing of books, after the Front and Back of the book jackets, the Front Flap is considered the most important. The Front Flap copy may be likened to a movie advertisement. It tells enough about the book, in quick, breathless prose, to make the reader want to buy it and peruse the pages. When students are assigned to write their Front Flap copy, tell them to "pull out all the stops." There is no room for humility or modesty here. Tell them to lay it on thick and heavy, with plenty of adjectives and superlatives and loaded with action verbs.

You could read the first few sentences from two or three of the Front Flaps of published books you have chosen as examples, or read the Front Flap copy presented in the outer column.

The Back Flap

We finally come to those precious words, ABOUT THE AUTHOR AND ILLUSTRATOR. No modesty needed here either. Now students have the opportunity to tell what fascinating people and terrific authors and illustrators they are. They may also mention their favorite activities and hobbies. Above all, they should have fun writing about themselves.

As examples, read three or four *About the Authors* from your example books, or read the one in the outer column.

The Spine (or Backbone)

This space is for labeling the book in such a way that the reader can find it after it is placed between other books on a shelf.

The Spine contains three pieces of information:

1. **Name of Author** (usually only the last name, because fiction books in libraries are arranged in alphabetical order by the author's last name);
2. **Title of the book** (typed or printed in the style that is used on the Front); and
3. **Name of the Publisher.**

Now assign the students to:

1. Design the Backs of their book jackets;
2. Write the copy for the Front Flap;
3. Write the copy for the Back Flap; and
4. Design the Spine.

Now allow them to work on those remaining four elements of their book jackets. At the close of the session, assign them to complete all four elements of their book jackets before returning for the next session.

SESSION 11

In the first part of this session, the editors should read and edit their writers' Front Flap and Back Flap copy. Then the art directors should review the Front and Back of their illustrators' book jackets, offering suggestions for improvement or words of praise. These two activities should not require more than thirty minutes. Then you should collect all edited Flap copy (both Front and Back) to review at a later time. Make sure students' names are written on all of their work.

How To Mark Off the Book Jacket Paper

Now distribute to each student a sheet of book jacket paper which measures 25½ inches by 11 inches.

Have them place the widest dimension across their desks:

BOOK JACKET PAPER

11″

25½″

SUGGESTED LESSON PLAN

Teacher Preparation:

Reread all of Session 11.

Materials Needed:

Book jacket paper

Art supplies

Rulers

Glue

Cardboards (for templates)

Activities:

Measure and mark book jacket paper.

Review all illustrations and text with layout of text sheet.

Time Required:

45 minutes

Assignment:

Review all elements of their books and make necessary improvements or alterations.

Neatly number pages 0 through 15.

Have them measure in from each side, 4 inches, and then draw a vertical line on each side:

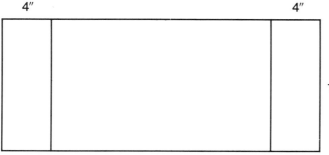

Now have them line up their cardboard template next to the line drawn on the left and draw a line on the right side of the template:

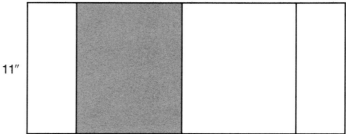

Now have the students line up the cardboard template on the line drawn on the right side and draw a line on the left side of the template:

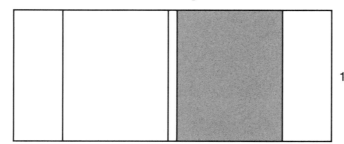

Once the lines are drawn, the book jacket paper should be divided into five parts, which measure as follows:

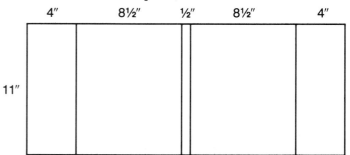

Instruct your students to write their names on the sheets, then have the sheets collected to be stored by you until the next session. Return their Front Flap copy and About the Author copy to them and tell them these should now be typed on their sketchpad paper or drawing paper in preparation for final assembly. Remind them that the size of both Flaps is 4 inches wide by 11 inches deep.

Caution students that they should take special care of all of their finished pages so that the pages are not soiled, torn nor wrinkled.

You should have about twenty minutes left in this session. We will not waste a minute.

Last Twenty Minutes of Session 11:

Have your students retrieve their printed layout sheets from their notebooks, then tell them their home assignment for tonight is to carefully review all their illustrations and their typed pages, making sure the pages are all properly labeled, **0 through 15.** Instruct them to write the numbers, neatly in pencil, within the margins of their finished pages. Example at left.

If by chance or mistake a student has an extra page, he or she should not panic because we have one fail-safe page, labeled F, reserved at the bottom of the layout sheet. This extra page may be used for that additional page, if necessary. Otherwise, page F is used as a Closing page.

If a student is short a page, it is even simpler to rectify. He or she can always add one more illustration.

Expanding and Exploring the Visual Images

Opening and Closing Pages

The opening pages of a book are the **Half Title** page and a two-page **Title** page. In books of considerable length, there is often a Table of Contents. However, since the body of your students' books consists of only sixteen pages, there is no need for such a Table. You might want to at least mention that the reason for a Table of Contents is to assist readers in locating chapters or main sections.

SESSION 12

SUGGESTED LESSON PLAN

Teacher Preparation:

Reread all of Session 12.
Make copies of Layout Sheet for Opening and Closing pages.

Materials Needed:

Art supplies

Activities:

Discuss elements of Title pages.
Begin work on Title pages.

Time Required:

45 minutes

Assignment:

Complete Title pages.

Title Pages

Instruct students to look at the two pages marked D and E on the Layout Sheets.

The Title pages contain the same information as does the Front of the book jacket:

    1. Title of book;

    2. An illustration;

    3. The line or lines, "Written and Illustrated by"; and

    4. The name of the author/illustrator.

PLUS — the Title pages contain **one more** piece of information — the **name of the publishing company** which the group has already chosen.

The job of the book designer is to adapt the type style and the design elements of the Front cover to the two-page spread of Title pages D and E, incorporating the name of the publishing company.

LAYOUT SHEET FOR OPENING PAGES AND CLOSING PAGES

Title _____ Illustrator _____

OPENING PAGES

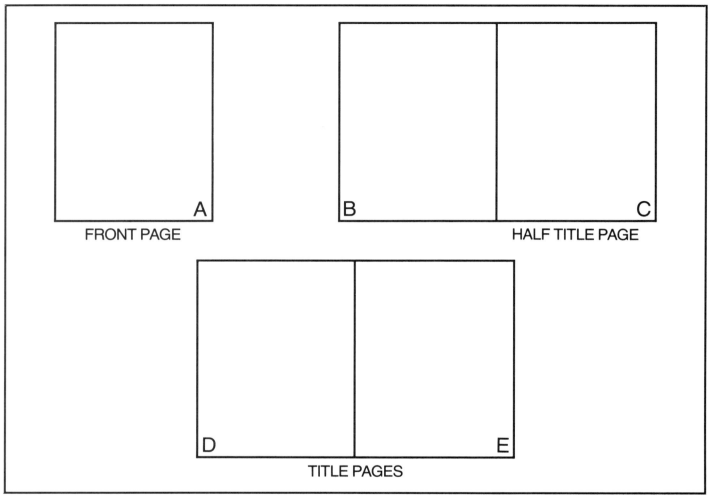

FRONT PAGE

HALF TITLE PAGE

TITLE PAGES

CLOSING PAGES

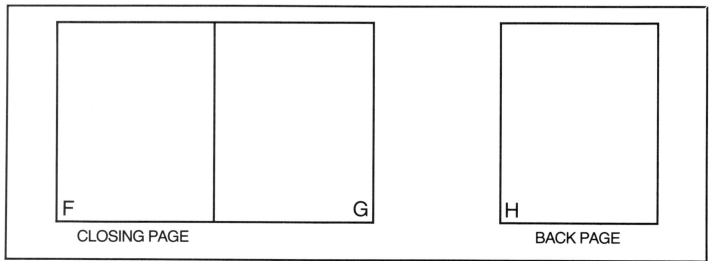

CLOSING PAGE

BACK PAGE

Students may lay out their Title pages in one of two ways:

ONE (the simplest way):
   Create a full-page illustration on page D, and place all the lettering on E:

Kathy Myers

Jeannie Dilger, 12

TWO:
   Students may trim two sheets of sketchpad or drawing paper and place the sheets side by side. Now they can design the illustrations across both D and E:

Kaye Anderson.

Bill Tolle, 13

— Janet Moody, 14

Rosanna Jalbuena, 12

   Instruct students to design and complete Title pages D and E and bring them to the next session.

SUGGESTED LESSON PLAN

Teacher Preparation:

Reread all of Session 13.

Materials Needed:

Art supplies

Activities:

Have students show Title pages to class and offer suggestions for improvements.

Discuss Half Title page and Closing page information.

Allow time for them to begin work.

Time Required:

45 minutes

Assignment:

Bring all typed pages and elements of book jackets to class, ready to assemble.

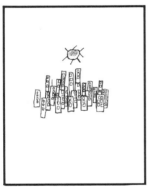

I LIKE NEW YORK
— Whitney Freas

THE WEDDING OF THE YEAR
— Ann Knopps, 11

It's *show-and-tell* time again. Hold up the students' two-page Title pages and solicit the class to offer suggestions for improvement.

Ten minutes will provide plenty of time for suggestions and the "oohs" and "ahs."

Half Title Page

Once the Title pages have been designed, the composition of the Half Title page is a snap, because the Half Title is a condensation of the Title pages.

Kevin Smith, 12   Melaney Lewis, 13   Angie Ferguson, 15

The Half Title page might contain only the title of the book and/or a small illustration:

If your students would like to dedicate their books to someone, suggest they leave enough space in the center of the Half Title page for the dedication to be typed.

Now allow your students thirty minutes to design and work on their Half Title page.

Closing Page

At least ten minutes before the end of the session, tell students they will need one more page for their books — a Closing page.

The Closing page usually consists of no more than a small illustration or design which is in keeping with the style of the book.

You may tell them that they might think of the element they design for the Closing page as an "ornamental period," used to punctuate the end of their book project. Label the Closing page F.

Assignment for the night: Review all of their pages once again to make sure each and every page is labeled in the lower margin of the page,

Students should now have completed pages, typed and/or illustrated, and labeled C, D, E, 0, 1, 2, 3, 4, 5, 6, 7, 8, 9, 10, 11, 12, 13, 14, 15, and F.

Students are to bring all typed pages and elements of the book jackets — the Front, Back and both Front and Back Flaps — to the following session.

Everything should now be ready for the final steps — the assembly and binding of their completed books.

Tom Gardner

A Rush to the Finish —the Excitement Builds!

Setting Up the Assembly Line

As you move into the assembly and binding phase of book construction, you will also need a maximum of table space on which the students may lay out their pages for the gluing and sewing processes. Many teachers arrange for their class to use the cafeteria for these sessions or an area in the library or a multipurpose room.

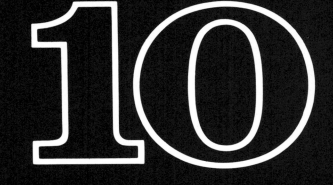

SESSION 14

SUGGESTED LESSON PLAN

Teacher Preparation:

Reread all of Session 14.

Materials Needed:

Book jacket paper

Glue

Scissors

Activities:

Have students trim all elements of their book jackets and glue them on the marked sheets.

Time Required:

45 minutes

Assignment:

Review all pages and make final corrections on all book pages from A to H and from 0 through 15 and bring them to the next session.

Listen Very Carefully

In every phase of book development, I have emphasized ways and means of making students switch to their creative brains. No more. From this point on, we want no creative brain activity. We want the absolute attention and concentration of the students' academic brains.

Any *creative* numbering or labeling could ruin their books. All labeling and numbering **must be precise and accurate.** Your instructions must be followed without deviation.

At the opening of this session, I tell my students:

"I will only say this one time, so you must listen very carefully.

"From this point on, you must listen to every word I say and follow every instruction to the letter. If you don't, you can now ruin all the work you have done on your books."

Pause.

Then repeat:

"From this point on, you must listen to every word I say and follow every instruction to the letter. If you don't, you can now ruin all the work you have done on your books."

Pause.

Then repeat once more.

Jeannie Williams

Brian Otto, 12

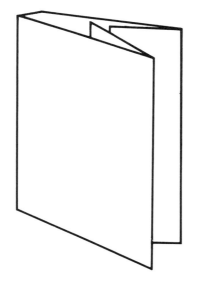

Assembly of Book Jackets

Using their cardboard templates, have students make sure the Front and Back of their jackets are accurately outlined.

Then instruct them to check the outlines of their Front Flaps and Back Flaps. The Flaps should be four inches (4″) wide and as tall as their books.

Now instruct your students to very carefully and accurately cut along the outlines with scissors and trim off the excess paper of the Front and Back. Then trim both Flaps.

If you have paper cutters available, you may wish to form an assembly line and trim the pieces — your choice.

As soon as everyone has trimmed all four elements, then give them the jacket sheets they had measured and marked during the previous session.

Have them check once more to make sure their jacket paper is properly labeled as instructed:

BACK FLAP	BACK	SPINE	FRONT	FRONT FLAP

Paste-up of Covers

Instruct the students to glue the Front on the area marked on their book jacket paper, carefully and neatly lining it up with the drawn lines and the edges of the sheets, then press it flat. They should take enough time to assure that their Front lines up exactly, but should move quickly enough so that the glue does not become too dry to stick.

Once the Front is glued in position on the book jacket paper, using the same process, have students glue their Backs and adhere them to the sheet.

Next have them glue the Front Flap and place it in position. Then glue and place the Back Flap.

Once all four pieces are in position, instruct your students to design and print in the information required on the Spines of their jackets — AUTHOR'S NAME, TITLE and NAME OF PUBLISHING COMPANY.

Now have them fold their jackets on the drawn lines so that each section folds inward, as illustrated in the outer column.

Next have them stand the jackets on a table or shelf and allow them to dry.

When the jackets are standing together, their appearance should cause excitement and delight. You and the students should feel a sense of achievement. It is now obvious that you are in the publishing business.

While it may seem these instructions for paste-up of the jackets are oversimplified and could have been given to your students for assembly at home, I assure you that by doing them in a group, you have saved the destruction of at least one jacket, probably more.

DO NOT ALLOW THE STUDENTS TO TAKE THEIR JACKETS HOME. YOU STORE THEM FOR SAFEKEEPING.

There should be enough time left in the hour to have the students retrieve their layout sheets from their notebooks for a quick review and additional instructions.

Instruct them to be sure to bring all elements of their books to the next session.

Tell them to label three of the pages in their sketchpads (or three pages of drawing paper), which they have outlined, H, A and G.

ASSIGNMENT:

Tell them to be sure they have all pages finished and properly labeled before the next session. Suggest that, at home, they lay out their pages on a table or a clean floor, in the exact positions as they are shown on the layout sheet. This will be their last opportunity to alter or improve any of their work. Then they should place all the pages together neatly and bring them to the next session.

THEY ARE NOT TO TRIM ANY OF THE PAGES NOR GLUE THEM TOGETHER IN ANY WAY UNTIL YOU SHOW THEM THE PROCESS!

FAT PHYLLIS
— Christine Steiger, 12

SESSION 15

Folding and Labeling Signature Sheets

Pass out the 17″ x 11″ signature sheets. Each student will need six. **Instruct the students to carefully fold each sheet in half:**

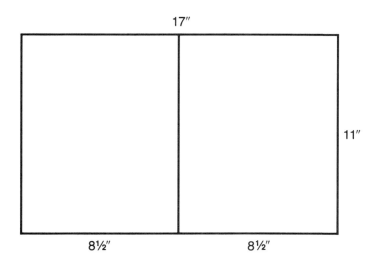

17″

11″

8½″   8½″

Now have students take out their rulers and pencils. Instruct them to place their rulers on the fold of the top sheet and draw a line on the fold.

SUGGESTED LESSON PLAN

Teacher Preparation:

Reread all of Session 15.

Materials Needed:

Signature sheets—17″ x 11″ (six per student)

Pencils

Rulers

Activities:

Show students how to fold signature sheets and draw a line on the folds on both their Fronts and their Backs.

Tell them how to gather, label and number the pages.

Have students review Opening, Text and Closing pages, and have them begin trimming finished pages.

Time Required:

45 minutes

Assignment:

Trim all pages and bring them to the next session.

Then have them draw the center line on the folds of all six sheets — on both sides. These lines will assist as guidelines for the positioning of the pages for gluing. The lines should be dark enough so they may be easily seen:

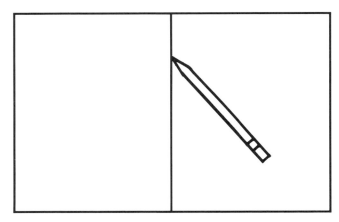

By opening the pages slightly at the center spread, students should be able to place the folded sheets over one arm like a saddle and none of the sheets will fall out:

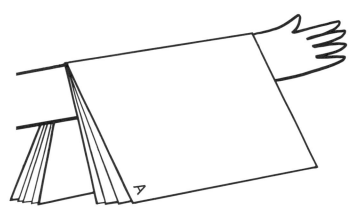

Tell them to label the page in the lower right-hand corner in pencil, boldly enough so they can easily see it and neatly enough so they will have no trouble reading it. Label the first page — A:

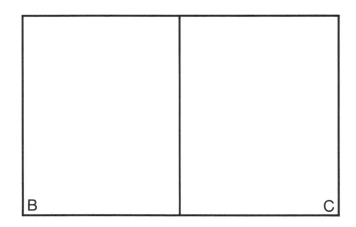

Now tell the students to insert the sheets together — like a magazine:

Now have them place the folded sheets on their desks as they would view a magazine — the pages opening at the right:

Now have them turn the pages as they would a magazine and label the lower corner of the left-hand page B and the right-hand page C:

Then turn the pages, one by one, and label them, as below:

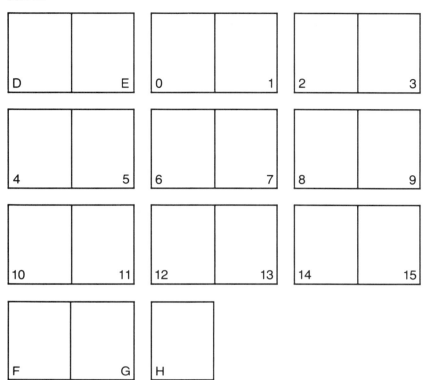

D	E

0	1

2	3

4	5

6	7

8	9

10	11

12	13

14	15

F	G

H

THE GODDESS STANDS GUARD
— Kathy Owens, 11

Have them write their names on Page A.

Then you should collect all the folded signature pages and keep them for the next session.

Trimming the Pages

Instruct the students to review all their prepared pages — opening, text and closing — to make sure they are properly labeled and that the lines made with the template are neat and correct.

Once students are positive all pages are finished, tell them to trim each page neatly, neatly, neatly along the border with scissors. Encourage them to take their time. You should watch carefully to make certain any student who has problems with manual dexterity or eye-hand coordination receives necessary assistance.

I FEED THE BIRDS
— Donna Van Doorn

 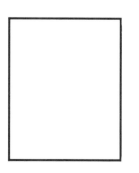

Before the close of the session, tell students to have all their pages properly trimmed before the next session and to be sure to bring all elements of their books to class.

FRIDAY THE THIRTEENTH
— Thomas Culhane

SESSION 16

SUGGESTED LESSON PLAN

Teacher Preparation:

Reread all of Session 16.

Schedule cafeteria or multipurpose room, if possible.

Materials Needed:

Folded, marked and labeled signature sheets

Glue

Scissors

Activities:

Show students how to paste trimmed pages on signature sheets.

When completed, gather pages in proper sequence.

Time Required:

45 minutes

Assignment:

None
(unless some students have not completed their paste-ups).

HE'S MY EAVER
— Jean Kaardal

Final Countdown

If you have the whole cafeteria at your command, each student can have a table to use. But if your work space is limited, everyone may have to take turns.

Again, warn the students that in gluing and assembly processes, they must listen carefully and follow your instructions exactly, because if they deviate from these instructions, in a matter of minutes they run the risk of ruining their books.

Some of the students who have followed every instruction up to this point, for some strange reason, will suddenly start pasting up their books with no regard for the numbers or markings. When instructed to trim their pages, some students who have done the neatest work will carelessly start whacking their pages with scissors, making the edges as ragged as a saw.

Pass their folded and labeled sheets back to them.

Have each student hand the folded sheets to his or her art director. The art director's job is to check the sheets, one by one, and make sure all pages are lettered and numbered correctly. Then the sheets are handed back to the author/illustrator.

All of this should take no more than five minutes.

Paste-up of Pages

Point out to students that when gluing their pages onto the folded sheets, only pages 6 and 7 will be glued in consecutive order. This procedure guarantees, in final binding, that all pages will be in the proper sequence. The individual pages which are labeled and numbered in the bottom margins **MUST** be glued onto the corresponding lettered or numbered page on the folded sheet.

Tell them to separate the folded sheets and arrange them on their tables in the order shown below:

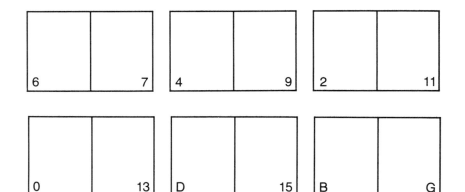

Now tell them to glue the pages in corresponding order, from 6 to G, left to right, as the sheets are laid out. The sides of the pages should not touch the center line of the folded sheet.

As soon as the students have finished gluing these pages, have them turn over all the folded sheets in the order shown below:

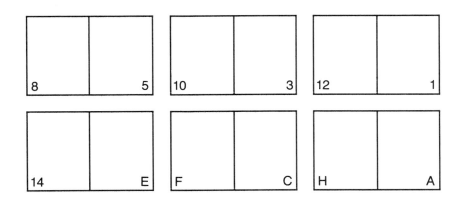

8	5
10	3
12	1
14	E
F	C
H	A

Now instruct the students to glue the pages in their proper places from 8 through A.

Gluing on Covers

Now distribute two sheets of cardboard and instruct the students to glue them to the pages labeled A and H, lining the top edge of the cardboard with the top of the page and *barely* missing the drawn center line, as shown below:

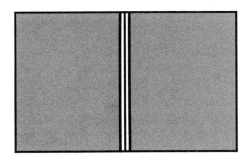

After the cardboard is glued into place and everyone has finished, instruct them to stack the pasted spreads on top of each other, in the following order:

Leave spread 8-5 as is;
Place 10-3 on top of it;
Now place 12-3 on top of 10-3;
Now place 14-E on top of 12-1;
Now place F-C on top of 14-E;
and finally, the spread with the pieces of cardboard on top of F-C.

When the students close the pages on the folds, the pages will automatically be in the right order.

Again, if you find some students have difficulty in following directions or in manually handling the folding or gluing processes, you may have to help them individually.

Collect all your students' pasted pages from them and you keep the pages safe until the next session.

You may now tell them that during the next session, all books will be stitched and trimmed and the jackets will be placed on the books.

DARK HOURS
— P. J. Modrell, 12

HOW TO PLAY GOLF
— Kim Norris

His Father drives Tom to school and he spends his holiday. Until Christmas he carries a big book and library magazines.

The former has a big son like Tom Brown. His name is Mark. He never fights with the children who disturb him because he is a close friend of Tom Brown. Mark has a dog named Sally.

TOM BROWN
— Laurence Small

SKIING
— Janet Schadler

Optional Step — Making Covers

The making of book covers is a step I have eliminated in the five-day Workshops. Once the book jackets are wrapped around the cardboard pages, the students' books look completely finished. However, if you would like for your students to really finish their books in top order, instruct them to purchase a roll of self-adhesive shelf liner at the local dimestore, Wal-Mart, K-Mart or wherever. They may select a pattern design that is compatible with their book or choose a solid color. Since one roll is more than enough for one book, you could buy several rolls and have each student pay for the amount of liner he or she uses. Or together, two or three students may purchase a roll.

For gluing, follow the instructions on the liner paper. Some liner's adhesive must be moistened to activate the adhesive, some have contact glue.

Instruct the students to take the outside pasted-up spread of their books, which now has the cardboard glued to pages H and A:

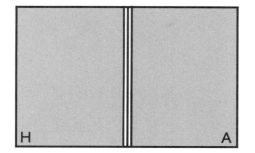

Now instruct them to unroll the shelf liner and lay their spread on the liner, leaving at least one inch to lap over the edges. Cut the liner neatly:

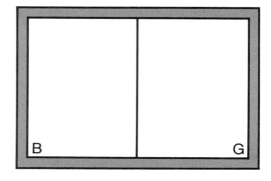

Now cut triangles out of outside corners and centers of the liner, as one does in wrapping packages:

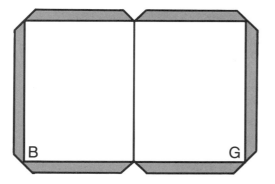

Then overlap the liner and adhere to pages:

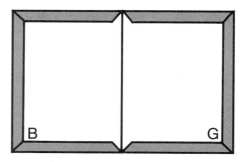

If contact shelf liner is used, the covers may be ready immediately.

But if moisture has been used to activate the adhesive, the covers should be laid flat, with weights placed on top, and allowed to dry overnight. Otherwise the boards will warp.

There is no doubt that the applied cover paper adds a certain elegance to the feel and the appearance of the books, but whether or not you have your students add shelf liner to their covers is your option.

Session 17

Binding of Books

Instruct students to make sure all pages are in the right order and lined up evenly at the top. Make sure all center-fold lines are lined up with each other.

Using a good-sized needle and carpet thread, have the students sew through all the pages, making stitches one-half inch apart. To make the sewing easier, use a thumb tack to make holes prior to stitching.

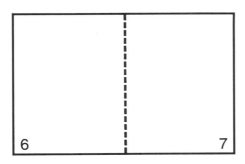

Tie thread and cut off excess. Now all the pages of the book are bound securely together.

Once the sewing is completed, have the students wrap their prepared jackets around their book covers and . . .

You Now Have Finished Books! Congratulations!

Everyone will want to look at everyone else's book and there will be an air of excitement, much like the day school yearbooks arrive. And rightfully so.

You and your class have accomplished what no New York publisher, with a staff of highly paid professionals, could achieve — in a period of two to three weeks, you have created and completed twenty to thirty original books!

You have made the world of literature richer.

Each book is unique — one of a kind. Each one is handmade, a rarity in today's world of mass production.

The books are precious items and valuable keepsakes. They are precious to you because you have been the catalyst in their creation. They are precious to the students — not one of them can help but have a sense of achievement after having created an original work of such quality. They will be precious to the parents. And if they are kept with the regard they should be awarded, these books will be precious to the future children of the students. And hopefully, years from now, someone will proudly take one of these books from a shelf and say, "My grandmother (or grandfather) wrote and illustrated this in school."

That thought always makes chills run up my spine.

As for now, do not let the students take their books home. At the end of the session, you collect the books for safekeeping.

Although the books are completed, the celebration of your students' creativity is only just about to begin.

SUGGESTED LESSON PLAN

Teacher Preparation:

Reread all of Session 17.

Materials Needed:

Needles

Thread

Thumb tacks

Activities:

Show students how to sew pages together.

Time Required:

45 minutes

Assignment:

Celebrate!

RAIN FOREST
— Eric Becker, 12

SAMMY SNOWPLOW
— Tammy Moyer, 12

Students Create Double-Page Delights

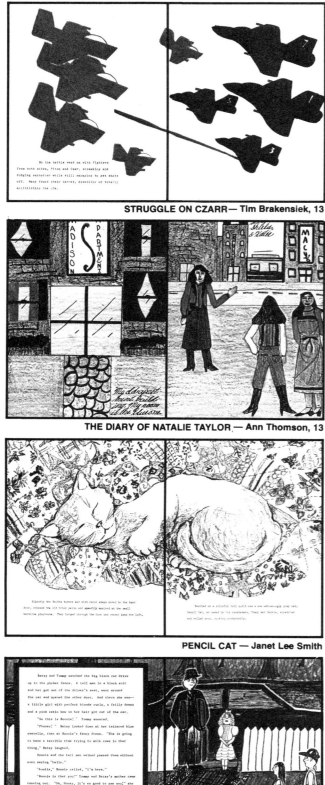

So the battle went on with fighters from both sides, Titan and Czar, streaking and dodging eachother while still managing to get shots off. Many found their target, disabling or totally annihilating the one.

STRUGGLE ON CZARR— Tim Brakensiek, 13

My deepest secret building. My room is the Union.

THE DIARY OF NATALIE TAYLOR — Ann Thomson, 13

Silently the Smiths turned and with rapid steps moved to the barn door, crossed the old brick patio and speedily arrived at the small barnlike playhouse. They lunged through the door and peered into the loft.

Nestled on a colorful tall quilt was a now not-so-ugly gray cat, Pencil Cat, so named by his caretakers, Tracy and Carrie, stretched and rolled over, purring contentedly.

PENCIL CAT — Janet Lee Smith

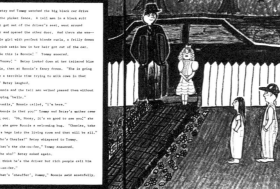

Betsy and Tommy watched the big black car drive up to the picket fence. A tall man in a black suit and hat got out of the driver's seat, went around the car and opened the other door. And there she was-- a little girl with perfect blonde curls, a frilly dress and a pink satin bow in her hair got out of the car.

"So this is Bonnie!" Tommy sneered.

"Phooey," Betsy looked down at her tattered blue overalls, then at Bonnie's fancy dress, "She is going to have a terrible time trying to milk cows in that thing," Betsy laughed.

Bonnie and the tall man walked passed them without even saying "hello."

"Auntie," Bonnie called, "I'm here."

"Bonnie is that you!" Tommy and Betsy's mother came running out. "Oh, Honey, it's so good to see you!" she said as she gave Bonnie a welcoming hug. "Charles, take Bonnie's bags into the living room and that will be all."

"Who's Charles?" Betsy whispered to Tommy.

"That's the cha-oo-fer," Tommy answered.

"The who?" Betsy asked again.

"I think he's the driver but rich people call him the cha-oo-fer."

"That's 'cheuffer', Dummy," Bonnie said scornfully.

BETSY'S REVENGE — Andrea Steiner, 14

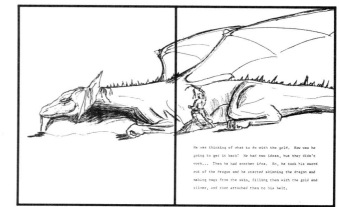

He was thinking of what to do with the gold. How was he going to get it back! He had two ideas, but they didn't work... Then he had another idea. So, he took his sword out of the dragon and he started skinning the dragon and making bags from the skin, filling them with the gold and silver, and then attached them to his belt.

THE DRAGON OF ORD — David McAdoo, 10

I sat driving into the darkness of the night, listening to the monotonous sound of my engine combined with the sound of my tires against the pavement. It could almost put a person to sleep while driving at night. I thought about the previous morning.

Jason drove into the parking lot and pulled in beside my red corvette already parked. He was late and he knew it. When he got out of his car, he walked quickly around to the trunk and started taking out luggage and equipment.

"You're late," I said, but got no reply.

-2-

ALMOST A LIFETIME — Scott Qualls, 13

So frantically swam out, realizing the sharks had eaten the bodies and they were probably ——————————————— the main source for the big crack on the bottom of the ship.

DEATH UNDER THE OCEAN — Mike Seward, 13

New York has lots of tall buildings. The tallest building in New York is the twin towers.

We have lots of Department Stores. The people during the summertime walk on the sidewalks looking in the stores.

I LIKE NEW YORK — Whitney Freas

WRITTEN AND ILLUSTRATED BY
ANDREW MARTIN

11

Books! Books! Books!
—the Goals Are Achieved

A Time for Celebration!

JOLENE HITS THE YELLOW TIDE
— Judy Nenninger

HORSES
— Enrique Carrancedo, 8

Several years ago, I attended a concert at Carnegie Hall in New York City to hear the Suzuki children play violins. All the girls were dressed in beautiful pink dresses, white anklets and patent leather shoes. They were so lovely — they looked like china dolls. The boys wore black slacks, white shirts and black bow ties — all very fitting for the elegant concert hall. At the end of the performance, as the Japanese ensemble began to play a closing number, ten American children, also playing violins, joined them on stage, then another ten walked on and another ten. This continued until the stage was filled with at least two hundred and fifty children. While the audience applauded the spectacle, I was appalled by the way the majority of American children were dressed. Many wore jeans and sweatshirts with printed advertisements for fast food chains or popular movie and rock stars emblazoned across their chests. Their choice of clothing would have suited sports events or a trip to a shopping center, but not Carnegie Hall. It saddened me to think our American children had the opportunity to stand on a stage where some of the greatest artists of the world had performed, yet they missed the experience of realizing the elegance that such an occasion should provide.

Elegant! Elegant! Elegant!

At the close of the WRITTEN & ILLUSTRATED BY...WORKSHOPS, parents and friends are invited to attend the unveiling of the students' books. At the ceremony, each student tells about his or her book.

I instruct students to hold up their books so the audience can clearly see them, announce the title, then give only a brief synopsis, not a page by page account, of the story. The ceremony lasts no longer than thirty to forty-five minutes.

Then refreshments are served — the more refined, the better. Serve high tea if you like. During refreshments, the authors' and illustrators' works are on display for all to see and they receive proper congratulations for their creative efforts.

THE KLUTZ
— Brian Haley

HERBIE FACES LIFE
— Angie Monteleone, 11

THAT'S HOW I WAS ADOPTED
— Patricia Witzenburg

— Katie Saab

The students should be dressed in their Sunday-best — suits, white shirts and ties for the boys, and for girls, their finest dresses — even evening dresses. Since they are celebrities, they may even don dark glasses if they like.

At your author/illustrator party, provide the most elegant setting and give your students the opportunity to dress for the occasion.

Public Relations and Publicity

Invite representatives from local newspapers and television stations to attend to interview the new authors and illustrators. Since the news media is quick to offer criticism of schools and their programs, now is their chance to write or show something positive. Be sure to contact them several days in advance. With very little effort, the WRITTEN & IL-LUSTRATED BY...WORKSHOPS have received wide news coverage in newspapers (often front page stories) and choice spots on evening television news shows. Since news reporters are vitally interested in writing, they have a built-in interest in students developing books. Once they see the outstanding books your students have created, they will indeed be impressed. And interviews with students provide wonderful human interest. People in the news media realize this.

Ways To Display the Books

Many of the books have been displayed in the windows of local department stores. Contact the manager or publicity director of a local store and such arrangements will be quickly made. The display of students' books provides wonderful public relations for stores and most stores are eager to show their interest in students' works.

Display the Books
in School and Public Libraries

Given the opportunity, most librarians will be eager to display your students' original books. Often they will provide an authors' party and invite people from the community.

Many librarians like to place the books with reference materials and check them out for those persons who would like to read them in the reference room.

How To Provide Other Enriching Activities
for Your Students

Many teachers would like to schedule time for one or several of your students (or all) to read their books to classes and to answer questions. These activities provide two-fold results: one, they offer your students opportunities to speak before groups; and two, such engagements encourage other students to write and illustrate books — in class or on their own.

The more ways you utilize the books to provide enriching experiences for your students, the more you will add to their self-esteem. Your students will develop new attitudes of self-confidence right before your eyes. It is a thrilling and rewarding experience for all.

12

Everyone Can
Write and Illustrate
Amazing Books

Special Considerations

NOTE: The examples of book covers and illustrations in this chapter do not include those done by brain-injured or learning-disabled students for specific reasons. Too often handicapped children and adults are segregated and pointed out as being different from the main. Refusing to add such insult to injury, their work is displayed throughout the pages of this book with no special designation made.

In order to protect myself from verbal abuse and even physical harm, I have not printed the ages of any of the adults. Since most of the handicapped students who participated in my Workshops have been young adults, their ages are not offered on the credit lines either.

In an earlier chapter, I said I would provide information about ways teachers might adapt the WRITTEN & ILLUSTRATED BY . . . WORKSHOPS to include younger children and those students who are neurologically impaired or learning-disabled.

I also mentioned earlier, although the Workshops were originally designed for students from ages twelve to seventeen, I have never had a group limited to just that age spectrum. Instead, I have groups of exceptions, and exceptions to those exceptions, ranging from six-year-old youngsters to seventy-year-old adults, and even groups comprised of brain-injured and learning-disabled children and young adults.

One Workshop at The Institutes for the Achievement of Human Potential in Philadelphia was composed of one adult, children as young as six years of age and a number of young adults who had suffered some brain injury. That group certainly presented a wide range of abilities, many superior to students their own age, some working at lower levels of development, but by the end of the Workshop, all had produced extraordinary books. I have since conducted two other Workshops at The Institutes, working with other exceptions to the exceptions. From my observations of these participants, I have drawn several conclusions as to how the Workshops can be adapted to suit the needs of younger children and those who have learning disabilities.

Younger Children

Six- and seven-year-olds write and illustrate books faster than do older children. Younger children have fewer inhibitions and will start writing and illustrating stories at the drop of a hat. Their work is prompt and direct. I had one six-year-old who really threw me a curve. When I assigned each child in the class to develop two illustrations within thirty minutes, she had completed ten illustrations and was looking for more paper.

Since younger children's writing skills are nowhere near their verbal

THE FLYING CAR
— Alison Myers, 5

THE CLOUD THAT COULDN'T RAIN
— Jason Sherman, 7

JACKIE
— Maureen Lawlor, 16

THE HOUSE THAT HAD NO FAMILY
— Robert Katzfey, 12

FREEWING, THE APPLE BLOSSOM VET
— Laura Harper, 11

skills and their abilities to make up stories, I found when I allowed them to dictate their stories to an adult, the structure of the plot and the development of characters were years beyond their spelling and printing skills, which is certainly no surprise to either teachers or parents. To accommodate the situation, we had a number of adult volunteers work as secretaries.

We also provided the younger children with extra assistance in all the mechanical aspects of book development, such as folding the paper and positioning the glued pages on the signature sheets.

In no way did we ever help them in developing titles or ideas for stories, or in choosing what media or colors they should use for their illustrations. I don't think they would have put up with such interference. Also younger children don't like to redo anything. They are really one-shot kids. When they draw an illustration, that's it. If you don't believe me, just try to convince one of them that the head on the cat should be smaller or that the whole drawing needs to be redone.

But given the proper assistance in the construction phases, younger children do produce. And they love the idea of writing and illustrating. From the word, "Go," they have no doubt they can do terrific books.

Working with Learning-Disabled and Brain-Injured Students

Working with learning-disabled and brain-injured students is much like working with younger students, except the teacher has to be even more observant and more flexible in the presentation of instructions and in giving examples. The teacher must also be able to recognize and emphasize the abilities of these students, rather than concentrating on their disabilities.

For instance, in the first group I worked with, the helpers and I drew all the outlines around the cardboard templates on the sketchpad pages. But when I worked with the second group, I allowed the students to try to use the templates and found, to my delight, that many could use them on their own while others needed only a little assistance.

Some in the group had little trouble writing their own stories. Others needed to dictate theirs. So I made sure we had enough volunteers to assist those who needed extra help.

As to the way I conduct these Workshops in comparison to others, there is very little difference, except that many of the students need secretaries. These students may also need more time to complete their books.

We have had amazing results with some of these students. During the course of developing a book, we often saw their skills in drawing improve by two or three grade levels. By having the experience of writing a book, we sometimes saw their thought processes become more complete in relation to their everyday activities. The mother of one of these students told me that after her son took the Workshop and had written a book, she received a letter from him. It was the first time he had written a letter that exhibited a straight line of thought processes and good solid information about his activities.

When conducted in an atmosphere of caring and sharing, by a teacher who is sensitive to any extra assistance they might require, I have no doubt that writing and illustrating books are wonderful activities for many handicapped students.

Afterword

Writers do not like to think their books end at the last page. After our books are read, closed and put back on the shelf, we would like to believe our words and thoughts will not be forgotten — that we have touched readers in some way, perhaps even improved their lives. Such is my hope for WRITTEN & ILLUSTRATED BY . . . !

I have no doubt that through encouraging groups of students to write and illustrate books, my life has been improved. On a special shelf in the back room in our house, we have more than one hundred handmade books which were duplicated by participants in the Workshops.

When I take THE ADVENTURES OF SIR SCOOPIN-POOP or MEPHISTOPHILES off the shelf, I am suddenly transported to the multipurpose room at Truman High School in Independence, Missouri. In my mind, I see that group so vividly that I could talk to them and walk straight to the tables where they developed their extraordinary books.

When I look at A GODDESS STANDS GUARD or SUPERFATS, I am again at Lindenwood Colleges in St. Charles, Missouri. I pick up ALBERT THE ARMADILLO or THE HOUND AND THE GOOSE and I'm in Houston, Texas.

When I hold in my hands THE DAY FOUR DOGS DIED or THE MAGIC DRAGON AND THE BRAVE UNI-CORN, I am once again standing in the auditorium of The Institutes for the Achievement of Human Potential in Philadelphia. Anytime I want a touching and fulfilling reminder, all I have to do is pick up any one of these wonderful books.

I can recall these students and places clearly because they were so charged with creative energy and enthusiasm. They have indeed left indelible marks on my memory. For whatever I taught these students, and, all modesty aside, I taught them a considerable amount, I have learned more from them than they could ever possibly learn from me.

In his book, EDUCATION AND ECSTASY, George B. Leonard proposes that a people is indeed fortunate if from kindergarten through college they have had three teachers who affected their lives in positive ways. I'm more fortunate than many — I can count at least twenty-three teachers who had major impact on my life. And since leaving school, I have had a series of people who have generously taught me additional skills and have provided me with a variety of insights.

When I review the twenty-three teachers who affected my life in positive ways, it strikes me that all had two qualities in common:

One, they saw possibilities in me I didn't know were there; and

Two, all of them made me switch brains frequently.

No matter what subject they taught — English, mathematics, world history, art or journalism, they constantly challenged both of my brains. They supplied precise information for the academic brain and were able to trigger the creative brain with insights and ideas, allowing me the opportunity to create and invent.

I suspect the teachers who affected your lives in positive ways had these same two qualities. I hope we, as teachers, strive to promote these qualities. By doing so, we may ward off the possibility of one of our past students someday returning to us, showing us an achievement and saying, "See, I was more than you supposed."

One evening during a Workshop, my daughter and I were editing the students' manuscripts. After Teresa finished one, she said quietly, "Dad, you've got to read this one next." I could tell she had been touched emotionally by the writing, and when I read the story I understood why.

In the book, HER CREATION, twelve-year-old Brenda Gelder tells a simple parable I wish all teachers and parents could read.

HER CREATION
— Brenda Gelder, 12

Once a little girl molded a piece of clay into a beautiful creation.

When the little girl tried to show it to her mother, she didn't have time to look.

When she tried to show it to her father, he was too busy to be bothered.

When she tried to show it to her grandmother, the old woman talked of other things and didn't look.

When she tried to show her creation to her teacher, the woman told her not to interrupt.

So carrying her creation into the woods, she offered it to the world.

Hoping someone would finally notice her marvelous gift, she hugged it and held it close to her heart.

This simple story should make us pause to wonder at the precious gifts of creation our students possess, and whether or not we have taken the time to encourage their creative endeavors.

Do I want every student in the world to write and illustrate a book?

Yes, I do.

Do I want all of them to become professional writers and illustrators?

I want all of them to become whatever they choose. My prime purpose is to allow students the opportunity to discover talents and improve their skills. I only want them to see the possibilities, then make their own choices.

So, in conclusion, I hope this book has no conclusion, but instead will open opportunities for new beginnings. It is obvious to me that as one person conducting eight WRITTEN & ILLUSTRATED BY . . . WORKSHOPS a year, I can affect the lives of no more than two hundred students in groups of twenty-five at a time. While each of these two hundred is important to me, I would like to see that number increase to two thousand or even better to two million. It is with this hope in mind that I pass this information and these methods on to you, and they are yours for the taking.

As you and your students create wonderful books, I hope you will take photographs and send copies to me. I also would be delighted to receive letters and newspaper clippings which tell of your success.

In a very short period of time, it is my hope that we can develop a national awards contest in which the outstanding books written and illustrated by students can be submitted for review and recognition, and that each year one book among these will be selected and published. This is my next goal. If you have ideas as to how we can achieve this goal, I would appreciate receiving your thoughts and advice.

My warmest regards
to you and your students,

David Melton
Landmark Editions
1420 Kansas Avenue
Kansas City, Missouri 64127

At Young Authors' Tea — with Enrique Carrancedo, age 8, the famous author and illustrator of the delightful book, HORSES.

David Melton
— author and illustrator

David Melton is one of the most versatile and prolific talents on the literary and art scenes today. His literary works span the gamut of factual prose, analytical essays, newsreporting, magazine articles, features, short stories, poetry and novels in both the adult and juvenile fields. When reviewing his credits, it is difficult to believe that such an outpouring of creative efforts came from just one person. In sixteen years, twenty-two of his books have been published, several of which have been translated into a number of languages.

Mr. Melton has illustrated ten of his own books and three by other authors, while many of his drawings and paintings have been reproduced as fine art prints, posters, puzzles, calendars, book jackets, record covers, mobiles and note cards and have been featured in national publications.

While most artists and authors develop a creative format which utilizes one particular style and approach, Mr. Melton adventurously searches for subjects that demand he adapt and create a unique and different style for each work. He insists that each of his books should have a distinct personality of its own.

Due to the versatility of his books, individually and collectively, they reach extremely diversified audiences of different ages and broad ranges of interest. The quality of his work has received enthusiastic acceptance and critical acclaim throughout the world.

Mr. Melton has also gained wide reputation as a guest speaker and teacher. He has spoken to hundreds of professional, social and civic groups relating the problems that confront parents and teachers of learning-disabled and handicapped children and has influenced the mandates of change in the fields of special education and therapies for brain-injured children. He is also a frequent guest on local and national radio and television talk shows.

Since a number of Mr. Melton's books are enjoyed by children, he has visited hundreds of schools throughout the country as a principal speaker in Author-in-Residence Programs, Young Authors' Days, and Children's Literature Festivals.

Mr. Melton also conducts in-service seminars for teachers and teaches professional writing courses throughout the country.

Other books by DAVID MELTON

Author:

TODD
Prentice Hall — Softcover, Dell Publishing
New Edition — The Better Baby Press

WHEN CHILDREN NEED HELP
T. Y. Crowell — Softcover, Independence Press

CHILDREN OF DREAMS, CHILDREN OF HOPE
With Raymundo Veras, M.D.
Contemporary Books

A BOY CALLED HOPELESS
Independence Press — Softcover, Scholastic Press

THEODORE
Independence Press

SURVIVAL KIT FOR PARENTS OF TEENAGERS
St. Martin's Press

PROMISES TO KEEP
Franklin Watts

Author and Illustrator:

I'LL SHOW YOU THE MORNING SUN
Stanyan-Random House

JUDY — A REMEMBRANCE
Stanyan-Random House

THIS MAN, JESUS
McGraw Hill

AND GOD CREATED . . .
Independence Press

HOW TO HELP YOUR PRESCHOOLER LEARN MORE, FASTER, AND BETTER
David McKay

THE ONE AND ONLY AUTOBIOGRAPHY OF RALPH MILLER — The Dog Who Knew He Was a Boy
Independence Press

HARRY S. TRUMAN — THE MAN WHO WALKED WITH GIANTS
Independence Press

THE ONE AND ONLY SECOND AUTOBIOGRAPHY OF RALPH MILLER — The Dog Who Knew He Was a Boy
Independence Press

Illustrator:

WHAT TO DO ABOUT YOUR BRAIN-INJURED CHILD
by Glenn Doman, Doubleday

GOOD-BYE MOMMY
by Bruce King Doman, The Better Baby Press — Encyclopaedia Britannica

IMAGES OF GREATNESS
Independence Press — Images of Greatness Commission

HOW TO BE YOUR OWN ASTROLOGER
by Sybil Leek, Cowles Book Co.

Designer:

HAPPY BIRTHDAY, AMERICA!
Independence Press

LANDMARK EDITIONS, INC.

HOW TO CAPTURE LIVE AUTHORS
And Bring Them To Your School
by David Melton

Especially written and designed to assist teachers and school librarians in developing and improving author-related programs.

Covers a full range of topics:
- Various types of programs
- How to schedule events
- How to contact authors
- How to finance programs
- How to prepare students and teachers for the occasions
- How to initiate related enrichment activities
- How to best obtain media coverage and promote public relations
- And more!

Complete with illustrations, photographs, suggested planning guides and organizational tips.

Compiled by an author with many years of experience in the field, with the assistance of numerous members of the International Reading Association and the American Association of School Librarians throughout the country.

8½" x 11" Softcover
96 pages   Retail price—$12.95
ISBN   0-933849-00-1

Prices subject to change without notice.